Summers at Shea

ALSO BY IRA BERKOW:

Summers in the Bronx
The Corporal Was a Pitcher
Full Swing
The Minority Quarterback
Court Vision
To the Hoop
The Gospel According to Casey (with Jim Kaplan)
How to Talk Jewish (with Jackie Mason)
Hank Greenberg: Hall of Fame Slugger (juvenile)
Hank Greenberg: The Story of My Life (editor)
Pitchers Do Get Lonely
The Man Who Robbed the Pierre
Red: A Biography of Red Smith
Carew (with Rod Carew)
The DuSable Panthers
Maxwell Street
Beyond the Dream
Rockin' Steady (with Walt Frazier)
Oscar Robertson: The Golden Year

Summers at Shea

Tom Seaver Loses His Overcoat & Other Mets Stories

Ira Berkow

Library of Congress Cataloging-in-Publication Data

Berkow, Ira.
Summers at Shea : Tom Seaver loses his overcoat and other Mets stories / Ira Berkow.
pages cm
ISBN 978-1-60078-775-1
1. New York Mets (Baseball team)—History. I. Title.
GV875.N45B47 2013
796.357'64097471—dc23
2012031637

This book is available in quantity at special discounts for your group or organization. For further information, contact:

Triumph Books LLC
814 North Franklin Street
Chicago, Illinois 60610
(312) 337-0747
www.triumphbooks.com

Printed in U.S.A.
ISBN: 978-1-60078-775-1
Design by Prologue Publishing Services, LLC
Page production by Patricia Frey

For Dolly

Contents

IV. A Clutch of Formidable Rivals

V. Why Baseball at All

Introduction

It is a fairly oft-told, but forever beguiling tale, more or less, of the first *Kiner's Korner*, the postgame interview program with Ralph Kiner that became iconic for New York Mets fans, and emblematic. It came about half an hour after the new-born Mets' first home game ever, on April 13, 1962, in which the team lost 4–3 to the Pittsburgh Pirates.

"It was a horrible place to work, cramped and dingy, in a room in the basement of the ballpark," recalled Kiner, in the spring of 2012, by phone from his home in Palm Beach, Florida. "Casey was my very first guest." The irrepressible Stengel was, of course, the manager of the Mets, which he called, "The Amazin's," but Amazin' how, was left to the imagination of the listener. (At one point in the season Stengel took note of his embryonic and hapless team, which went on to lose 120 games out of 160, for a major league record of ineptitude. "We have to learn to stay out of triple plays," he suggested. And famously, he was supposed to have asked, in exasperation, "Can't anybody here play this game?", which became the title of Jimmy Breslin's terrific book on the early Mets.)

"The show was going fairly well, but I hadn't done much TV before and was nervous and wasn't sure how to end the interview with Casey, who was a non-stop talker," continued Kiner. "So when I was getting waves to cut from my director, I said, 'Well, Casey, thanks for coming on....' Casey was experienced enough in interviews to know that it was over. He said something about, 'Glad to be here,' got up, and the lavaliere, the little microphone, was still clipped to his uniform, and he walked away, and pulled the whole damn set down."

The Mets, a team composed of castoffs from other teams, aging veterans, and not-quite-ripe young players, had opened the season in St. Louis, with a two-game series against the Cardinals. But the first game was rained out, and the Mets lost the other. "But before getting to the ballpark, the team got stuck on an elevator in the Chase Hotel," recalled Kiner. "Well, not the whole team, but about six or seven players. The rainout was one omen, this was another, and a pretty good introduction to how the season was going to go."

The Mets lost their first nine games, and at that point were actually 9½ games out of first! "The Pirates had won 10 in a row," explained Kiner.

That first Mets game was played in the Polo Grounds, the former home of the New York Giants, before they departed for San Francisco following the 1957 season, and it was to be the Mets' home field for two years, or until they moved into the newly constructed Shea Stadium, in Flushing, in the New York City borough of Queens.

The Mets' first game in Shea was played on April 17, 1964, before, perhaps, a fairly skeptical, sparse crowd of 12,447. Ironically, they lost to the same opponent, the Pirates, by the same score, 4–3, as they did in their initial opener in the Polo Grounds. A headline in *The New York Times* stated: "50,312 Attend Opener at Shea Stadium. Lack of Parking Causes Backups." Another omen.

I came to New York to work as a sportswriter for Newspaper Enterprise Association, a Scripps-Howard feature syndicate, in the late summer of 1967, and one of my first pieces took me out to Shea. The Mets were still "The Amazin's," in a less than august way, to be sure, and wound up the season in 10th place, 40½ games behind the National League pennant winners, the Cardinals. The next season, they improved to ninth place, 24 games behind, again, first-place St Louis. (So, in their first seven seasons, they finished 10th five times, and ninth twice.)

Then, in 1969, the Mets, behind a sensational young pitching staff, caught fire and, in midseason, went over the .500 mark for the first time in their history. They didn't stop there. They went on to catch the first-place Cubs, win the National League pennant, and play the heavily favored Baltimore Orioles in the World Series—and lost the first game, but went on to sweep the next four. The Amazin's—truly, stunningly, improbably this time—were baseball champions of the world.

I had the opportunity to report on the team and even to travel with them on their charter plane as they soared to the championship that season.

I continued to write about them, with the reporter's and columnist's access to the field and dugout before games, and the clubhouse before and after contests. I did so with NEA and then with *The New York Times*, until I retired from everyday journalism in 2007, a year before the Mets' last season at Shea, when they repaired to their new ballpark across the way, Citi Field.

So my summers (and springs and falls) at Shea coincided with nearly the entire history of the Mets in that ballpark (that is, 40 of the 45 years), and what I didn't get firsthand in the earlier years, I was able to write about when the occasions arose from interviews with those who were there, including Mets players and managers—and a broadcaster (after all, Kiner, in 2012, at age 89, was going into his 51st consecutive year in the Mets' booth, though at a reduced schedule of 25 games).

And while it is said that the drama and soul of a team and its players are often captured in the losing clubhouse—and there was plenty of that with the Mets—there was also the added pleasures and excitements of the winning, and striving to win, clubhouses. And there were enough of those for me—on hand, as it were, for the Mets' pennant-winning seasons of, besides the Tom Seaver–led 1969 "Miracle Mets," as they came to be called, the Yogi Berra–managed 1973 team (and Willie Mays' last season), the remarkable come-from-behind Gooden-Strawberry-Carter-Hernandez-Darling-Knight-Mookie- etc. 1986 champions, and the 2000 Subway Series against the Yankees, managed by, of all people, the Mets' former manager, Joe Torre.

The last game at Shea on September 28, 2008, saw the Mets, still in the thick of the pennant race, lose to the Florida Marlins, and swiftly go from thick to thin. That is, out of the race altogether. Following the game, and the end of their season, the Mets held a "Shea Good-bye" tribute. A good number of former players from the Mets' glory years entered the stadium, toed home plate one final time as the fans politely and, surely, forlornly stood and applauded their once-upon-a-time heroes. The ceremony concluded with Tom Seaver throwing a final pitch to Mike Piazza as "In My Life" by The Beatles played on the stadium speakers. The two former Mets stars then strode across the Kentucky bluegrass, walked out of the center-field gate, and closed it behind them. A display of blue and orange fireworks followed. It wasn't long after that the wrecking balls arrived to tear down the old ballpark.

In the years at Citi Field, the Mets have been disappointing on the field and suffering terrible problems in the front office. Though their payroll has been one of the highest in baseball, they have not been consistent, at best, and blew several first-place division leads down the stretch to fall out of contention.

Some of the Mets' acquisitions, like second baseman Luis Castillo and pitcher Oliver Perez, did not pan out. Star pitcher Johan Santana, acquired via trade in 2008 and then re-signed to a six-year, $137.5 million contract, suffered injuries in each of his first four years, including one to his rotator cuff that required surgery and caused him to miss all of the 2011 season. The inability to pay Jose Reyes, their league-leading-hitting shortstop, what he got to sign as a free agent with the Miami Marlins following the 2011 season further depressed the Mets' fandom. And the trials, literal and figurative, of the team's highest executives, co-owners Fred Wilpon and Saul Katz, in the midst of the Bernie Madoff Ponzi scheme scandals—were they or were they not "willfully blind," as the legal term has it—were a distraction, to say the least, for Mets fans. (On March 19, 2012, they day on which they were scheduled to go to trial in the case, the Mets owners settled the federal lawsuit brought against them by Irving H. Picard, the trustee for the victims of Madoff's scheme, for $162 million. Picard, in turn, dropped all claims that Wilpon and Katz were involved in wrongdoing in the eyes of the law. In the complex resolution, Wilpon and Katz may wind up paying not even a fraction of the settled amount.)

But back to baseball:

"Losing a 7½-game lead with 17 games to play in 2007," recalled Mets fan Paul Golob, a Manhattan book editor, "was but one of the painful periods in recent years. I could go on."

"One aspect of going to a Mets game is seeing how long you waited at Shake Shack for refreshments," said Mets fan Maddie Korf, a New Jersey middle-school teacher. "On line you usually hear people saying that they don't care how long they'll be there, because they're not missing anything on the field anyway."

And *The New York Times* op-ed columnist David Brooks wrote a column on March 8, 2012, titled, "Hey, Mets! I Just Can't Quit You." Living in Washington, D.C., this longtime Mets fan had thoughts of transferring his baseball team allegiance to the local Washington Nationals, but then cited current players like "hustling" outfielder Daniel Murphy, "charming" first baseman Ike Davis, and "funny" knuckle-baller and mountain-climber R.A. Dickey. (Not to mention outfielder Lucas (Camptown Races) Duda):

"...The project to switch to the Nats has been a complete failure.... I've come to accept that my connection to the Mets exists in a realm that precedes individual choice. It is largely impervious to calculations about costs and benefit. It is inescapable.... It's probably more accurate to say that team loyalty of this sort begins with youthful enchantment. You got thrown together by circumstance with a magical team—maybe one that happened to be doing well when you were a kid or one that featured the sort of heroes children are wise to revere. You lunged upon the team with the unreserved love that children are capable of."

And, as Paul Golob and Maddie Korf would surely agree, one continues to inevitably follow the team and hope for the best, year after, often, disappointing year. Though dim as it may be, a rainbow remains in their mind's eye.

For the sportswriter, however, you seek to keep your fandom checked at the turnstile and/or at the writing machine—typewriter once upon a time, laptop today. I'm from Chicago, and so the Cubs were my boyhood team—well before the Mets were a gleam in anyone's eye.

My job, however, as a columnist and feature writer, primarily—as opposed to a beat writer covering the game itself—was to give a sense, a feel of "being there," to write about elements of the on-field participants that the spectator is not aware of, and cannot be aware of from his vantage in the grandstands, or on a couch in front of his television set. When, for example, I drove with Ron Darling—him behind the wheel, me in the front passenger seat—on the morning of Game 7 of the 1986 World Series, a game in which he was to be the starting pitcher for the Mets against the Boston Red Sox, a game that probably was the most important of his career. I hoped to capture his thoughts and whatever his anxieties were as he motored in the morning rain up the East River Drive to Shea Stadium.

So, this is that book. They include pieces I did for NEA, from 1967, and for *The New York Times*, from 1981. It is not an encyclopedic chronicle of events, nor meant in any way to be all-inclusive, but rather an eclectic rendering of some of the people, and some of the times, in the life of the Mets. Except for some very minor fixing of syntax or fact, the pieces are presented in real time, essentially transporting the reader back to those moments. I hope they meet with the reader's approval.

Something else I'd like to add. In many ways, Casey Stengel, the inimitable first manager of the Mets, remains a presence with the team. And his uniform number, 37, is retired and honored with its representation on the Citi Field outfield fence. I once met with Casey, then 83 years old, in a Manhattan hotel room and had an idea to do a historical, instructional baseball book with him. "Let me think about it," he said. "I'll let you know."

About two weeks later, in February, 1974, I received a letter from him. It was written in a firm but uneven hand on lined notebook paper. The letter was in blue ink, though the envelope was written in green ink. The envelope, which was personal stationery, announced at the top left:

> Casey Stengel
> 1663 Grandview
> Glendale, California 91201

The letter read exactly as follows:

> Dear Ira:
>
> Your conversations; and the fact you were the working Writer were inthused with the Ideas was Great but frankly do not care for the great amount of work for myself.
>
> ;Sorry but am not interested. Have to many propositions otherwise for this coming season.
>
> Fact cannot disclose my Future affairs.
>
> Good luck.
>
> (signed) Casey Stengel
>
> N.Y.Mets & Hall of Fame.

And so, naturally, I begin this Mets book at the beginning, with Charles Dillon (Casey) Stengel.

I.

FROM CASEY TO ACTUALLY AMAZIN'

"STAINED-GLASS" CASEY STENGEL

August 2, 1968

CASEY STENGEL SAID HE recently celebrated his 78th birthday. The baseball record book says it oughta be 79. No matter. Casey is one of those rare birds who never grows old. That's because he's never been young.

For proof, note the following account by Damon Runyon of how Casey Stengel, then 33 (or 34), hit an inside-the-park home run in the ninth inning to win the first game of the 1923 World Series, 5–4, for the Giants over the Yankees:

"This is the way old Casey Stengel ran yesterday afternoon, running his home run home....

"*His mouth wide open.*

"*His warped old legs bending beneath him at every stride.*

"*His arms flying back and forth like those of a man swimming with a crawl stroke.*

"*His flanks heaving, his breath whistling, his head far back.*

"Yankee infielders passed by old Casey Stengel as he was running his home run home, adjuring himself to greater speeds as a jockey mutters to his horse in a race, swore that he was saying 'Go on Casey! Go on!'"

Runyon added that Stengel's "warped old legs...just barely held out" until he reached the plate. "Then they collapsed," wrote Runyon.

Three thousand miles away in California, Edna Lawson, Stengel's fiancée, proudly showed newspaper clippings of Casey's game-winning blow to her father. "What do you think of my Casey?" she asked.

Her father shook his head. "I hope," he said, "that your Casey lives until the wedding." Edna and Casey were married the following August, and Casey's warped old legs even made it up the aisle. ("For the bridegroom," Casey said at the time, "it is the best catch he ever made in his career.")

Casey Stengel sat in the New York Met dugout at Shea Stadium prior to the recent old-timer game there. If accounts by Runyon and others of his day even border on accuracy, then Casey has not changed appreciably. If he could run a home run home then, he could probably do it now, too.

His white hair is sun-tinged in spots. A wave flaps over the side of his face, which is wrinkled like a rutted road. His blue eyes water now and then and he wipes them with a handkerchief as big as a flag. His tasteful blue suit is specked with light brown, and looks almost natty on him.

And his legs. Of course, his warped old legs. He crosses them at the knee and one works nervously under black executive socks. On his feet are black slippers. A young man wonders if old Casey Stengel wasn't shod in them when he ran his home run nearly half a century ago.

Old friends greeted Casey. Younger fellows introduced themselves to a legend in the parchment flesh. Some players that played for Casey when he managed the Amazin' Mets dropped by to chat briefly. And Casey talked. Someone has described Everett Dirksen as having a "stained-glass voice." If that is so, then Casey's voice is cracked stained-glass. And his syntax is as cloudy as rubbings from time-worn church-yard tombstones.

About the lack of hitting in the majors this year, Casey said: "They ask you, you ask yourself, I ask you, it's them good young pitchers between 18 and 24 years of age that can throw the ball over the plate and don't kill the manager, isn't it?"

About the St. Louis Cardinals: "St. Louis can execute and do more for ya. I thought Baltimore was going to be something but I quit on 'em and then I thought Pittsburgh would excel but I quit on them, too.

"But you gotta admit they can run, St. Louis I mean. Yeah, we'll say they can run. And they got two left-handers who'll shock ya and now the right-hander is commencing to be like Derringer or some of the others was. And a three-gamer, too. Can pitch every third day. The center fielder is a helluva good player and the left fielder is doin' an amazin' job. The fella at third they always worry about but he's doin' everything anyone could want. The first baseman got lotsa power and the catcher's now throwin' out people."

An old sportswriter friend came by and said he had just seen Edna in the stands and she's looking as great as always.

Old Casey Stengel, who ran a home run home nearly half a century ago, jumped up on those warped old legs in black slippers and grabbed the old friend's hand.

Stengel's gnarled face beamed. "You got it, kid," he said, pumping the man's hand. "You sure do."

CASEY STENGEL THE VAUDEVILLIAN

February 1, 1974

"EVEN THOUGH BABE RUTH ran me out of vaudeville," said Casey Stengel, "I still can't knock him."

"Now this fellow in Atlanta is amazing. He hits the ball the best for a man of his size. But I can't say he hits the ball better than Ruth. Ruth could hit the ball so far nobody could field it. And that's even with the medicinal improvements today. They come along now with the aluminum cup and it improves players who only used to wear a belt and it's better for catching ground balls."

Stengel jumped up on his bowed, lumpy, but still spunky 84-year-old legs and hounded down an imaginary ground ball that bounded under the coffee table.

"I got an offer from Van and Skank, the biggest names in vaudeville—they were from Brooklyn—to go on the stage after the 1923 World Series.

"I hit two home runs to win two games in that Series. I hit one in the first game and one in the third game. And this was when I was with the Giants and the Yankees were already the Yankees with Babe Ruth.

"Now, I remember Ruth when he was a young pitcher with the Red Sox. I batted against him, and this was before he grew the barrel on his belly but he always had those skinny legs. Well, they figured they could make more money with him in the lineup every day instead of every fourth day so they moved him first to first base but they had a good fella there so they moved him to outfield.

"In that series I hit an inside-the-park homer to win the first game. I was 33 years old. And I had a bad heel so I wore a cup in my shoe. The cup started comin' out when I was roundin' the bases. All the pictures show my like this"—head with hunk of white hair thrust back—"and like this"—head flung forward, rheumy blue eyes wide, tongue thrust out from his deeply stratified face—"and puffin'."

"So then the vaudeville guys asked me, could I sing. Sure I can sing"—for this voice sounds like cracked stained glass—"and can I dance? Sure. They wanted to pay me a thousand dollars for a week. And I wasn't making but five thousand—maybe six thousand—for a season playing ball.

"I was riding high. But the Yankees and Ruth said, 'Better watch out,' after I got the home run. It was a threat to brush me back. In the third game I hit a homer over the fence to win the game. And I ran around the bases and I made like a bee or a fly had got on the end of my nose and was bothering me. I kept rubbing it with my thumb, and sticking my five fingers in the direction of the Yankee bench...Commissioner Landis fined me for that.

"So I began to practice my dancing and I thought I'd be the new Fred Astaire. But then Ruth hit three home runs in the last game and the Yankees won the Series and vaudeville forgot about me and nobody heard from me again for 10 years.

"So now Ruth, he could have gone on vaudeville. Hell, he could have gone to Europe. It was near the end of my career and pretty soon I commenced managing. Ruth kept on hitting homers. Aaron is going to break his record, and so the National Broadcasting people asked me to talk for three minutes about Aaron being better then Ruth. I couldn't say that.

"It's a livelier ball today, and Aaron was up more times. And they use the fake fields, and the balls whoosh through faster. But Aaron is amazing the way he can hit 'em with his wrists.

"Now, Ruth struck out a lot. But any damn fool knows that nobody pays to see the world's greatest singles hitter. Or the world's greatest doubles hitter. Ruth was the world's greatest home run hitter and that's what everybody wanted. And that's what he gave 'em.

"It worked out okay for me, too. Because I'm still in baseball—vice-president of the New York Mets ballclub and in the Hall of Fame—and who knows what my future in vaudeville would have been. Just like I started out to be a dentist. The dean of my school said, 'Why don't you be an orthodontist?' That way I could have got a lot of rich kids and put a black filling in their mouth.

"The dean said, 'Always try to be a little different.' And today I make speeches all over. People ask me, Casey, how can you speak so much when you don't talk English too good? Well, I've been invited to Europe and I say, they don't speak English over there too good, either.

"So you can see why I can't knock Babe Ruth, even though he drove me out of the vaudeville business, can't you?"

CASEY GONE BUT STILL BAFFLING

September 14, 1976

CASEY STENGEL LEFT MORE than a great baseball legacy when he died last September 29. What also remains is his estate worth $40 million. Casey went out in characteristic fashion, however, leaving a financial plight that is as inscrutable and transcendent as Stengelese.

Two wills of Stengel's exist. One was signed in 1932. The only person mentioned in it who's alive today is his wife, Edna. Now in her 80s, she is hospitalized and legally certified as mentally incompetent.

The other will was drawn up in 1971. A number of would-be beneficiaries are still alive and relatively lucid. The problem is, Casey never got around to signing that document.

The courts must decide where Casey's shares in banks, stocks, oil wells, and real estate will go, and who gets his cash. Rather, who gets some of his cash.

"There are about 35 keys to safe deposit boxes that no one can find," said Herb Normal, the New York Mets' equipment manager and friend of Casey's since Stengel was the club's manager in the early 1960s.

"As I understand, letters were sent out to all the banks within a 100-mile radius of Casey's home in Glendale, California, asking if these keys belonged to any of their boxes. So far, nothing."

Stengel died at age 85, and for most of his public life—he became a major league outfielder in 1912 and managed many teams, most notably leading the New York Yankees to an unprecedented 10 pennants in 12 years, 1949–1960—he was considered a clown or a genius or a treasure. Or all three.

If there was anything he understood nearly as well as baseball, it was money.

He was vice-president of a bank in Glendale, of which his brother-in-law and executor, John Lawson Sr., is chairman of the board.

As Casey got older and—if possible—more prolix, some nieces and nephews, according to Herb Norman, tried to declare him mentally incompetent as well.

"Once," said Norman, "Casey handed me a satchel and said to hang on to it for a while. I tossed it in my locker. For some reason, I looked in the satchel. It was loaded with bundles of cash! I counted up to $35,000!

"When I saw Casey I said, 'Why did you do that to me?' He said, 'Because I trust you.' I said, 'But why didn't you tell me?' He said it was part of a business deal and wanted to keep it quiet since he didn't want family after it. I said, 'But what if it were stolen?' He said, 'So what.... By the way, take some.'

"The family situation landed in court. And the judge ruled, 'Casey, you're saner than I'll ever be.'"

Casey knew how important money was for his players and, when they deserved it, would go to bat for them with owners over salary.

Elston Howard, when a young Yankee catcher, was asked to make a trip to Japan with the Yankees one winter. He said he couldn't because his wife was expecting a child. Casey felt it was important Howard go for the playing experience, and told Howard to call his wife a few times a week from Japan and bill him.

"And I'll never forget one night we're having a party in Osaka and there's a phone call for me," said Howard. "It's my wife. She had the baby. Stengel had put in the call for me. It was a total surprise. Those phone calls altogether must have cost over $200. But I was grateful."

One of the players Stengel most respected was the Met infielder Rod Kanehl. Rod had little ability but played with gusto. After Kanehl finished his career, he was having a rocky time. Stengel sought to get him a job in baseball. At one Old-Timers' Day game at Shea Stadium, Kanehl, trying to be funny, began to rag Stengel.

"Hey, you old geezer," said Kanehl, "you made all your money from your old man watering down whisky in Kansas City." Apparently, there was some truth to Stengel's father's business, but not necessarily to how Stengel astutely amassed his own fortune.

Stengel grew ashen. "I've got money, you don't," said Stengel. "You're trying to get a job, I'm not. Don't ever ask me to do anything for you again."

This reporter had occasion to speak with Casey about money matters a few times. We sat in a dugout one afternoon several years ago. He was nearly 80. His face was as wrinkled as an old elephant hide. His blue eyes were watery, and he wiped them with a red handkerchief as big as a flag. The ears were floppy. His voice was rumbly and his syntax cloudy as rubbings from old tombstones.

I asked why the Los Angeles Dodgers were such a successful organization. Casey said, "You know the owner is smart because he keeps the seats clean. If you wear a clean dress it'll stay clean when you sit down. He runs a public park and he's not going to be arrested for being neat about it. And you know he's kept Alston ever since he got him. So that's number two on how you know how smart the owner is."

Stengel was noted for having an incredible memory, except for one blind spot. Names of people. He often mixed them up. Herb Norman remembers that when he and Stengel began working together, the old manager kept calling him "Logan."

After a month, Norman went into Stengel's office. "Casey," he said, "my name is not Logan. My name is Herb Norman."

Stengel looked at him with that gnarled, gremlin face, and said, "Do I make my checks out right for you?"

WARREN SPAHN AND CASEY, BEFORE AND AFTER

November 26, 2003

IN THE SPRING OF 1942, a 20-year-old left-handed pitcher who wound up having no decisions in his four appearances with the Boston Braves that season was pitching in an exhibition game against the Brooklyn Dodgers. At one point Boston manager Casey Stengel instructed the young pitcher to brush back the batter, Pee Wee Reese. He refused.

Stengel immediately dispatched the pitcher to the minors, to Hartford of the Eastern League.

"Gutless," Stengel said of him.

The next year, 1943, the pitcher enlisted and found himself in Europe with the Army's combat engineers in World War II. He participated in the savage Battle of the Bulge and the seizure of the bridge at Remagen, and when it was over, First Lt. Warren Edward Spahn was awarded a Purple Heart for a shrapnel wound and a Bronze Star for bravery and a battlefield commission.

"I said 'no guts' to a kid who wound up being a war hero and one of the best pitchers anybody ever saw," Stengel said. "You can't say I don't miss 'em when I miss 'em."

He added, "It was the worst mistake I ever made."

Indeed, Spahn, determined and talented, became one of the best pitchers ever. Though he didn't win his first major league game until 1946, when he was 25—he missed three baseball seasons when he was in the military—he pitched until 1965, when he was 44.

He won 363 games, more than any other left-hander, and posted a record of 23–7 and a 2.60 earned-run average in 1963, when he was 42. He was elected to the Baseball Hall of Fame in 1973, the first year he was eligible.

In the last of his 21 big-league seasons, Spahn pitched a part of the year for the Mets, a last-place team, with Casey Stengel as manager, after Stengel's great years with the Yankees. When Spahn played for Stengel and the Braves, the team finished in seventh place.

"I played for Casey before and after he was a genius," Spahn said.

Warren Spahn died Monday, at age 82, at his home in Broken Arrow, Oklahoma.

In the mind's eye, I can still see that quirky kick when he was about to fire a baseball homeward, looking as if he were trying to step over a fence about eye high, a delivery that led to his two no-hitters after age 39 and to his 13 seasons with 20 or more victories. He holds the National League home run record for pitchers with 35, and in 1958 with Milwaukee, he joined those pitchers who won 20 games (it was 22) and hit .300 (.333 to be exact) in the same season.

The last time I saw him was in August in Cooperstown at the Hall of Fame induction ceremony. When he was introduced to the audience along with the other Hall of Famers, he appeared from behind a curtain wheeling himself in a wheelchair. He was frail, his hawk nose looked larger than ever on his thin face, but he was there, resolute as ever.

There were times when the old competitor could be curmudgeonly, but as Murray Olderman, who covered baseball in New York in the 1950s and '60s recalled, "He was just fine once you got to know him." In his last season with the Braves, Spahn's manager, Bobby Bragan, accused him of selfishly hanging on for the salary. When he was with the Mets, Stengel thought he was getting a player-coach, but it turned out Spahn was interested in only pitching. When he was out of the big leagues the next season, he couldn't get pitching out of his blood, and played in Mexico.

Jerome Holtzman, the longtime baseball writer, admired Spahn's intelligence, and recalled he had a good eye for the dollar. "They had a Warren Spahn Day in Milwaukee and one of the presents was a tractor, for his farm in Oklahoma," Holtzman said. "Spahn had it shipped to Oklahoma, and billed the Braves."

Spahn's death came on the day the Arizona Diamondbacks agreed to trade Curt Schilling to the Boston Red Sox, meaning that Schilling, who has a full no-trade clause, may end his career in the city in which Spahn began his. Interesting to compare the two pitchers. They have similarities: classy performers, winning pitchers, strikeout aces. The differences, though, are great.

Schilling, 37, has pitched 16 seasons in the big leagues and has 163 victories. He has won more than 20 twice. He would need 20 victories a season for the next seven seasons to reach 300. Schilling, among the most successful of his era in pitching complete games, has 79 in 338 starts, 23.4 percent; Spahn's record dwarfs Schilling's, with 382 complete games in 665 starts, for 57.4 percent, more than double Schilling's percentage.

Spahn's career reflects something more than the ultimately superficial aspects of the game, like whose uniform one wears, or the winning or losing of a baseball game, or a championship. It is the tale of one man's grit to remain confident, calm, and poised—even though, surely, suffering doubts and fears—in the face of disappointment on the mound. He also displayed valor in a foxhole.

Spahn made 14 All-Star teams and helped pitch three Braves teams into the World Series, the first in 1948. That season, the Braves were in a heated race with the Cardinals and the Dodgers for the National League pennant. Coming down the stretch, the team's two best pitchers, Spahn and Johnny Sain, performed superbly under pressure. Spahn, particularly, was no stranger to pressure.

The *Boston Post* ran a poem by its sports editor, Gerry Hern, that captured the moment as well as leading to a widely quoted phrase:

First we'll use Spahn, then we'll use Sain.
Then an off day, followed by rain.
Back will come Spahn, followed by Sain,
And followed, we hope, by two days of rain.

AN ORIGINAL MET GOES BACK IN TIME

September 28, 2003

A PITCHER WHO HASN'T appeared in a major league game in 39 years, and had compiled a persevering 29–62 record to show for his eight seasons with the Reds and the Mets, received a mention Tuesday on the front page of *The New York Times*' sports section.

It appeared in a chart titled "Amazin' Race," which depicted the Detroit Tigers' gritty attempt to break the modern record of 120 losses in a season, held by the inventive 1962 Mets—inventive in that, as their manager, Casey Stengel, had said, "They've shown me ways to lose I never knew existed."

In Game No. 156, *The Times* reported Tuesday, the "1962 Mets lost, 7–3, to Braves. Pitcher Jay Hook set N.L. mark with team's 71st wild pitch," for its 117th defeat of the season. (The Tigers, after the same number of games, had nudged ahead with 118 losses, an American League record, but then won three straight in the last week of the season in a valiant effort to avoid the mark.)

"Well, I guess it's always good to be acclaimed for something," Hook said by telephone the other day from his home near Traverse City, Michigan. He is retired, at age 66, after nearly four decades as an executive in the automotive industry and as a professor of industrial management at Northwestern University. "When I look back on that year with the Mets, I think, 'I wish I—we—could have done better.' Funny thing, but when we lost, we always thought, 'We'll win tomorrow.'" He laughed.

"I must have been the supreme optimist."

In fact, he didn't do as poorly as his record of eight victories and 19 losses for the expansion Mets might indicate. Two other pitchers on the staff, Roger Craig and Al Jackson, lost 20 games or more. Hook, who was the winning pitcher in the Mets' first victory, after the team opened the season with nine straight losses, wound up with a 4.84 earned-run average, and a lot of his losses were hardly his fault.

Take loss No. 100 that season, on August 29 at Philadelphia. Hook pitched into the 10th inning with the score 2–2. A crucial play occurred with two outs in the fourth inning when third baseman Charlie Neal threw to first to try to get Don Demeter. The throw pulled Marv Throneberry off the bag. (Marvelous Marv, remember, was the man Stengel said he had wanted to give a cake to for his birthday but figured he would have dropped it.) Anyway, Throneberry snared the throw, went to tag Demeter, slipped, and fell flat on his face. The Mets went on to lose, 3–2.

Hook, who lives some four hours north of Detroit, has been watching the exploits of the 2003 Tigers on television.

"Some people had said to me, 'Don't you hope the Tigers break the Mets' record, so you don't have to live with that anymore?'" Hook said. "The answer is no. Not for our sake, for their sake.

"You see, our team had a lot of veterans, guys like Gil Hodges, Richie Ashburn, Frank Thomas, and Roger Craig, who had been successful in the major leagues and had a lot of winning seasons. And we had a lot of young guys who were just starting out. Casey himself had won 10 pennants with the Yankees before coming to the Mets. So a lot of reputations were established.

"The Tigers are a different story."

This is true. In Detroit's case, however, it also has to be a combination of abominable upper management and lamentable luck.

"I feel bad for Alan Trammell," Hook said. "This is his first year as a manager, and he was a terrific player, a winning player. But they don't have a lot of veteran players, and they have mostly young guys. And I can see how they lose focus.

"There was a game against Kansas City several nights ago in which the Tigers came back to tie the game, 4–4, in the fifth inning. But then the young pitcher gets ahead of the batter and, instead of making him try to fish for something low and outside, comes in high, and the batter pounds it. And the Tigers fall behind, and lose. I hate to second-guess, but maybe with experience, in a year or two, this won't happen."

It seemed the Tigers looked defeated. This wasn't the case with the Mets. Hook said, "We never thought we were that bad, probably because of the veterans."

Hook, a hard-throwing right-hander at 6'2", 180 pounds, was 25 when he joined the Mets, having been picked up as a "premium" choice in the expansion draft from Cincinnati.

When he was with the Mets, Hook spent off-seasons in graduate school studying engineering, with a concentration on gas (or automotive) dynamics. He could elucidate Bernoulli's Law, which explains why an airplane can take off and, with its "velocity gradations" and "force vectors," among other points, also explains how a curveball curves, which Hook once did at his locker at the request of a reporter.

Stengel called Hook "Professor." After a game in which he was knocked out of the box in the fourth inning, Hook genially recalled that Casey came by his locker, looked at him, and said, "If Hook could only do what he knows."

In 1962, he knew enough to start 34 games and complete 13 of them.

"I had to laugh the other day when I heard an announcer in a game say that the Toronto pitcher, who had won 21 games, had a chance to complete his fourth game of the season," Hook said. "Most starting pitchers don't go past six innings these days.

"My wife, JoAnn, pointed out to me recently that pitchers with the kind of record I had today are making two and three million dollars a year. I was making twenty thousand. But they were different times."

Hook added: "When I think about the Tigers, I'd like to tell them that this isn't the end of the world. A lot of the guys from the 1962 team went on to successful careers beyond their playing days, some managed big-league teams, some did well in business. And they have to understand that tomorrow is a new day."

Jay Hook—Professor Hook—was growing ever more philosophical. "In the world of life," he said, "it's only a baseball game."

For the 2003 Tigers, however, it was baseball game after baseball game after—uh-oh—another baseball game.

PIGPEN HUNT AND HIS ODD TALENT

July 1, 1987

NOBODY IN THE SPRING of 1975 trained harder or weirder than Ron Hunt, who held the major league record for being hit by the most pitches in one season, 50, in one career, 243, in one extra-inning game, 3, and for leading the league in being hit by pitches in consecutive seasons, 7.

"They may be dumb records," Hunt had said, "but they're the only ones I got."

Hoping to make it into his 13th big-league season, Hunt, a burly 6-footer who was then 34 years old, trained with the Cardinals in St. Petersburg, Florida. Ron Hunt training for a season was like no one else training for a season.

The Cardinals, like all teams, had a pitching machine named Iron Mike, which is programmed to hurl baseballs plateward. Iron Mike hit nobody, other than Hunt.

"I guess he's not got my number, too—caught me six times already," explained Hunt one morning that spring.

But isn't it unusual for Mike to bop anybody?

"I don't think about it," Hunt said. "He's got his problems, and I've got mine."

Hunt, who actually practiced getting hit by pitches, would be released at the end of spring training, and his black-and-blue career came to an end.

But last Sunday the name of Ron Hunt surfaced again when Don Baylor of the Boston Red Sox was whomped by a pitch for the 244th time in his career, breaking Hunt's major league record.

In some seasons, Baylor and Hunt each got hit more times than the combined totals for almost all of the other teams in those seasons. "It's crazy," said Baylor, when he was about to tie the single-season mark of 24 for the American League a few seasons back. "I don't know if it's a record to be proud of."

"I think it's great," offered Hunt, speaking by telephone the other day from his home in Wentzville, Missouri. "I'm glad Baylor broke the record. I was hoping to find someone dumber than me."

That's a figure of speech, certainly. Hunt, known in his day as Scrap Iron and Pigpen for his, well, gritty style of play, used the hit-by-pitch as an effective weapon, just as Baylor has done. It's a way to get on base especially when the pitcher has, say, an 0-2 count and, as Baylor says, "You're two-thirds struck out."

It began for Hunt when he was the second baseman for the early Mets, and Casey Stengel, at the end of his rope, offered $50 to the first Met to drive a runner in with the bases loaded by getting himself plunked by a pitch.

Hunt won the $50, and more after that. In the light of strange records, it may be forgotten that Hunt was a fine player for much of his career, with a .273 career batting average.

In 1963 he was second to Pete Rose for National League Rookie of the Year. Yet Hunt was a man born for those Mets. He received at his apartment a bouquet of flowers after a good game that rookie year—and sneezed, he says, for a week afterward. Rough Ron is allergic to blossoms.

In 1964 he became the first legitimate Met All-Star, and the first true hope of their future. He started that year in the All-Star Game. And got hit by a pitch.

He also played in the 1966 All-Star Game, and, as luck would have it, got hit again.

He was traded to the Dodgers in 1967, and to the Giants in 1968. In San Francisco he began to perfect the art of being nailed by pitches.

"I studied the rule book," he said, "and it said that you have to make an attempt to get out of the way of the ball. I practiced in front of a mirror. I lined up everything right at where the corner of the plate would be, my shoulder and elbows and hips and ankles, and then twisted toward the catcher. I didn't move out of the way, but I moved. That's an attempt."

From 1968 through 1974, including stints with the Expos and the Cardinals, he led the league in being hit each season.

He passed the career record of 195. "It was held by...," Hunt hesitated. "Who was that guy who hung over the plate all the time? Minoso. Yeah, Minnie Minoso."

In 1971, on Hunt's record-shattering single-season 50th hit-by-pitch, the Cub hurler, Milt Pappas, argued that Hunt was struck by a strike, but to no avail.

Pappas then turned his venom on Hunt. "I hope it hurt good," he shouted.

Hunt said nothing. "I didn't want to add insult to injury," he recalled. "Besides, I don't talk to pitchers."

Hunt gloried in his bruises. "Getting hit by pitches kept me in the league a few more years than I mighta stayed," he said. "Drysdale, Koufax, Gibson, Seaver, Ryan, Bunning. You name 'em, and I been hit by 'em."

Hunt looks with disdain at the recent instances of batters charging the mound when hit by pitches. "I never charged the mound," he said. "Never knew who all was hittin' me on purpose, got hit so many times."

Which pitcher hurt him the most? "Whichever hit me the most," he said. "They all hurt."

In later years, Hunt found that wearing a rubber vest, or flak jacket, inside his uniform shirt helped his game, and improved his health. "I cheated a little," he admitted.

These days, Hunt runs a business consulting firm, has a farm with cattle, and manages a touring team of teenagers called the Independents. And he still plays in old-timers' games.

On Sunday, while Baylor was establishing the hit-by-pitch record in New York, Hunt was letting no moss gather around him. He played in the old-timers' game in Montreal and got pinged by a pitch.

"I still get hit all the time," he said. "I lead the old-timers now."

THE METS 20 YEARS LATER

April 14, 1982

SHERMAN (ROADBLOCK) JONES, AMID snowflakes, was the starting pitcher for the original Mets in their home opener in 1962 in the old Polo Grounds.

Yesterday, at Shea Stadium, under sunny skies, he was the designated honoree—survivor, as it were—to memorialize the 20th anniversary of the Mets' entry into the National League. It was a team that would be recorded as the worst in baseball history and, as hopeless underdogs, one of the most adored.

As yesterday's game was about to begin, a late arrival in the press box at Shea Stadium, taking his seat, turned and asked a colleague, "Where did Roadblock throw out the first ball from, the boxes or the mound?"

"He hasn't thrown out the first ball yet," said his companion. "Oh," came the reply, matter-of-factly, "they probably can't find him." Well, they did. The old Mets used to get lost a lot, sometimes they couldn't find the ballpark, often they didn't have the foggiest where first base was.

But the 1982 Mets aren't anything like the 1962 mob—or weren't yesterday. On that April day two decades ago, Roadblock pitched the Mets to their first of 120 losses—they won 40—but yesterday the Mets were stunning, whipping the Philadelphia Phillies and Steve Carlton, 5–2. Goodness gracious, maybe, as the house ads would have us believe, the magic is back.

They have a new manager, George Bamberger, and a new slugger, George Foster, and, off this one game, anyway, a new élan. They displayed the fine touches that produce not just winning baseball, but interesting baseball. They hit with men on base (particularly Dave Kingman's three-run homer in the fifth), laid down the sacrifice bunt when it was called for (Bob Bailor's in the seventh was a beauty), and made the outstanding fielding play (see Hubie Brooks' stop at third base with two on and two out in the eighth) when anything less might have ended, as it had in past years, in catastrophe.

And the pitching held up, particularly the starter. Randy Jones, no relation and not necessarily an heir to Roadblock, gave the Mets five good innings and gave the Phillies just one run; he departed only after a 35-minute rain delay had, presumedly, stiffened his arm.

It was the Mets' fourth victory in six games, and two of those have come over Carlton, the first in the Phillies' home opener. This is terrific business. Carlton is a marvel. The older he gets—he is 37—the stronger he seems to become. He is the leading left-handed strikeout pitcher in history—he now has 3,161, fourth overall behind Walter Johnson, Gaylord Perry, and Nolan Ryan—and last year he averaged 8.5 strikeouts per nine innings, the best of his career. He struck out seven Mets before departing for a pinch hitter after six innings, but he also allowed all five runs on seven hits, the biggest being Kingman's blast over the left-field fence.

Kingman received such an ovation then that, after disappearing into the dugout, he returned to wave his cap to quell his idolators. There were two other ovations of note. One was when Foster was announced in the pregame lineups, and the other was for Bo Diaz, who looked puzzled.

Diaz is the Phillies' catcher. He was scheduled to lead off the top half of the seventh inning. The game had already been delayed once—in the fifth—and rain had begun to fall again in the sixth. But when Diaz came out in the seventh, the fans broke into applause, for, simultaneously, Diaz appeared from the dugout and the sun reappeared from behind the clouds.

In the old days, with the Mets ahead, they would have booed the sun—and hoped for serious moisture to end the game before the Mets would kick it away.

Richie Ashburn remembered those days. He was one of the Phillies' announcers yesterday, but he was the Mets' center fielder playing behind Roadblock Jones 20 years ago.

Ashburn, 35 then, and at the end of his 15-year career, was one of the players—young and old—who were on their last legs for the 1962 Mets, an expansion team of castoffs and callow rookies.

"I was the leadoff hitter and I don't remember exactly what I did, but I know I made an out," he said, during the rain delay. "I guess I set the pattern. It's strange, but I had a pretty long career and finished with a .308 batting average. But the thing most people seem to remember is that I played for the worst team in history."

Ashburn recalls the last day of that season. "It was against the Cubs, in Chicago, and it ended on a triple play. In the clubhouse afterward, Casey tried to make us feel better after this disastrous season. He said, 'Fellas, don't feel bad—it was a team effort. No one or two guys could have done it alone.'"

Perhaps the highlight of that season was, said Ashburn, the day Marvelous Marv Throneberry hit a triple. "The story's been told before but it's absolutely true," Ashburn said, recalling an episode with Throneberry and the Met manager, Casey Stengel. "The bases were loaded and it looked like the game-winning hit. Marv goes sliding into third—it was like a dust storm. In the dugout, we saw Marv miss first base. But Casey didn't—he was too busy jumping up and down. The first baseman—I think it was Ernie Banks of the Cubs—asks for the ball, and tags first, and the umpire calls Marv out, and no runs count.

"Casey goes running onto the field, screaming that he's being robbed. Dusty Boggess was the umpire at second base, a nice old guy, and he puts his hand on Casey's shoulder and says, 'Casey, I hate to tell you this, but he also missed second base.'

"Casey looked at him for a moment, and said, 'Well, I know for damn sure he didn't miss third!'" For the current Mets, maybe the magic is back; for the Mets of 1962, however, the magic will always be there, black as it might be.

RYAN, PAIGE, AND RULES FOR KEEPING YOUNG

March 9, 1992

PORT CHARLOTTE, FLORIDA—THE ONLY time Nolan Ryan met Satchel Paige was in the mid-1970s in Los Angeles, and the old pitcher—now the late old pitcher—gave the young man a piece of advice. "One of the best pitches is the bow-tie pitch," said Paige.

Ryan looked at Paige, then about 70 years old. Ryan was close to 30 and already an experienced big-league pitcher, but he was puzzled. "What's a bow-tie pitch, Satch?" he asked.

"That's when you throw it right here," said Paige, drawing a line with his hand across his Adam's apple. "Where they wear their bow tie."

This was sound advice, Ryan believed, and he has not been above using the bow-tie pitch to keep batters off the plate and make them reluctant to dig in. Of course, Ryan's pitches remain bullet-fast, which also makes the batter wary, whether he's concerned about a baseball landing on his bow tie or not.

Last season, Ryan's 24th in the major leagues—his first five were with the New York Mets—he was still one of baseball's best pitchers. Among other achievements, he was third in the American League in strikeouts—adding to his career strikeout record, which stands at 5,511—and he flung his seventh no-hitter, three more than anyone else in history. Now, at 45, an age when most old ballplayers are home clipping coupons or out hooking drives, Ryan looks forward to yet another remarkable year on the mound.

While his hair is thinning, and there are the little crow's feet about the eyes, the rest of him looks pretty fit. "And my arm? My arm is just fine," he said the other day in the clubhouse here at the Texas Rangers' spring training camp.

Can he top the seniors' mark of Satchel Paige, who pitched in the majors when he was 47 years old?

"I don't know, but then no one really knows how old Satchel was," Ryan said. "He might have been 57. At least I have a birth certificate. And I have people who could verify it, though not as many as there used to be."

Ryan isn't certain why he has had such staying power—especially throwing as hard as he does at the age he is—but he believes genetics probably has something to do with it, as well as diet, exercise, and attitude. Ryan said he had once read Satchel Paige's rules for keeping young and thought at the time that they were "applicable" to him.

In the interest of public service and the field of geriatrics, enduring concerns of this column, Ryan was asked to comment on Paige's six famous points to promote health and longevity:

Paige: "1. Avoid fried meats, which angry up the blood."

Ryan: "I think from a cardiovascular standpoint, Satchel's right. I stay away from fried foods now, even though I grew up in Texas where a frying pan was always sitting on the stove. Nowadays I have my food broiled. I stay away from fatty foods, and chocolate cakes and chocolate pies, which I used to love. But I don't know anything about angrying up the blood."

Paige: "2. If your stomach disputes you, lie down and pacify it with cool thoughts."

Ryan: "I take naps when I can, and I always try to get seven or eight hours' sleep a night. You want to keep relaxed. I tried to teach my kids that. They've been around the clubhouse since they were little bitty tykes. And they've seen a lot. They've seen players get into fights, they've heard cussing, they've seen managers go crazy. I told them: 'That's not how we act. There are a lot of different type people in the world. But we're not like that.'

"Also, don't let things upset you that you can't control. And try to make any difficult situation better. Last season, for example, we brought up a rookie catcher, Ivan Rodriguez, and he caught me in his second game. We weren't in rhythm, because that takes time. But I set my mind beforehand not to get upset, and to work with him. So, I shook him off until he called the pitch I wanted, and it didn't throw off my concentration."

Paige: "3. Keep the juices flowing by jangling around gently as you move."

Ryan: "My assessment of that is, basically, stay loose by stretching. At this age, you tend to stiffen up when sitting in one place for too long." What about jangling? "Sure, if you know how to jangle. I'm not sure I do."

Paige: "4. Go very light on the vices, such as carrying on in society. The social ramble ain't restful."

Ryan: "Very true. You can do a lot of things with the body, but do everything in moderation." How does Ryan characterize "social ramble?" "Bar hopping, staying out late in a joint or something. Over-indulging. Listen to your body. Sometimes the rumble is because of the ramble."

Paige: "5. Avoid running at all times."

Ryan: "Here I disagree with Satchel. I think a pitcher needs to run to build up stamina and to strengthen the legs, the hips, the knees, the lower back. But I don't run for distance anymore, and maybe I run 40 percent of what I used to. The recovery rate to bounce back gets longer. If this keeps up, there's a good chance that when I'm 47 I won't be able to run at all. So, Satchel might be right again."

Paige: "6. Don't look back. Something might be gaining on you."

Ryan: "I take Satchel to mean that you can't start worrying now. You know there's always some kids behind you. Let them worry about it."

Then Ryan went over and climbed on the stationary bicycle. And one was reminded that Satchel Paige's exercise machine was also stationary. It was a rocking chair.

• • •

Nolan Ryan, who was 6–3 for the 1969 Mets, appeared in one game in the World Series, in relief, and was credited with a save in Game 3. Ryan, a future Hall of Famer, was traded by the Mets to the California Angels after the 1971 season for aging infielder Jim Fregosi—which turned out to be a stunningly unwise trade by the Mets.

PRESSURE IN THE PENNANT RACE

September 16, 1969

ST. LOUIS—NO HORROR-STRICKEN CRIES of "Put you pants back on! Put your pants back on!" reverberated through the New York Mets' clubhouse, as it did the night they beat the Cubs and owner Mrs. Joan Payson, a sweet, smiling cushy matriarch, unexpectedly came in to congratulate her team in the literal flesh.

No champagne gurgled now as it did after that September night the Mets took a doubleheader from Montreal and moved into first place for the first time in their brief but lamentable history.

Nor was there the somberness of the long days and nights when they were tumbling, it seemed then, from sight of the first-place Cubs. The same kind of sullenness, surely, that has marked the Cubs' clubhouse in recent weeks, and which can be found on a given evening in Los Angeles or Atlanta or Cincinnati or Houston or San Francisco when one of these contenders loses in the race for the pennant, the race for glory, the race for the loot.

The Mets were in the clubhouse preparing for another pressure game in the teeming heat of the stretch drive. There was some levity, as always, but there was also an air of purpose.

Jerry Koosman, wearing a Yoo-hoo T-shirt (the soft-drink company owned in part by Met coach Yogi Berra), was pitching that night. He tilted back in his chair and placed his feet with spiked shoes on the side of his locker.

"Mmmmmm, yeah," said Koosman, "I sure do feel the pressure of the pennant race. Like this morning, I'm coming down the elevator of the hotel with my roomie, Ron Taylor, and I say, 'Ron, I wake up the day I'm going to pitch and I want the day to be over. It goes so slow. I sit around and worry about how I'm going to do. Is this the pressure getting to me? Is it a lack of confidence?'

"Ron was with the Cardinals when they won pennants and he told me that it was just my way to get up for the game, that if I wasn't hung up like this I'd be overconfident. That would hurt."

Some players, like infielder Kenny Boswell, say, "It's like the first day of spring training and we're getting a big kick out of it."

But Donn Clendenon, long, leathery, whip-looking first baseman, thinks like Koosman.

"I was with Pittsburgh when we had a few runs at the pennant," he said, "and the pressure built pretty much like it is here. But we have to use pressure as a vehicle to motivate adrenalin. We've got to control it. We can't let it get to us the way it did the Cubs. You could see and feel that they were tense, that they weren't the same club they were for most of the season—two outfielders calling for the ball and it drops, hitters too anxious and swinging at bad balls."

Bobby Pfeil, rookie infielder, was saying how he feels the pressure: "I remember the other day between games of a doubleheader. We won the first. But there was no celebrating. We knew we had to win the second. I sat in front of my locker and I was eating a ham-and-cheese sandwich and drinking a Coke. Usually I finish it all. This time, I left half the sandwich and half the Coke."

The players now filed out of the clubhouse to warm up before the game. Only Cal Koonce, the pitcher, remained. He was being rubbed down by the club trainer. He looked dreamy, as men on rubbing tables often look. When the clubhouse man walked past, Koonce looked up and cracked the silence of his thought. "Say," he asked, "how many games do the Cardinals have left with the Cubs?"

STRETCH DRIVE

September 16, 1968

ST. LOUIS—NEW YORK MET shortstop Bud Harrelson, frail-looking with a gaunt face and light-blue catlike eyes, dug in in the batting cage, then cracked a clean hit which sounded very, very loud.

Outfielder Ron Swoboda watched intensely as he leaned against the cage with his jaw nestled in the crook of his arm. Mechanically, he would turn to spit out shells of polly seeds. Nearby, third baseman Ed Charles, waiting his turn, rested like a flamingo on his bat, outfielder Cleon Jones, who has a camel-bump rump, and catcher Jerry Grote were off to the side stroking line drives at imaginary pitches.

"It's so quiet around the cage now," said rookie outfielder Amos Otis, recently called up after spending the summer in the minor leagues. "That's the big difference. When I was up here before until June, there'd be a lot of joking. You know, like calling Ed Charles granddaddy and saying he should hit with a cane instead of a bat. But you can also feel the spirit getting higher."

"Now," Harrelson said later, "it is strictly work."

"Since we made our pennant surge," said Swoboda, "I've found that we all try harder when we're not playing. We take every pitch in the batting cage, for example, seriously. We concentrate all the time, where, if you're 50 games behind, we wouldn't."

"It's true," said manager Gil Hodges, "because a player on this club never knows when he'll be put in a game."

But Tommie Agee, for one, believes very little has changed. "There is always pressure, from April to September," he said. "That little thing"—pointing at a baseball in the corner of the batting cage—"is where the pressure is. You're always trying to run it down. You're always trying to put wood on it, you're trying to put leather on it.

"But this club is loose and we aren't going to panic down the stretch the way the Cubs have done, and not the way the White Sox did when I was with them in '67."

Then, Agee recalls, the Chicago White Sox were in first place by a game with five games left in the season. The five games were with the two tail-end teams, Kansas City and Washington. The White Sox lost all five and finished fourth.

"I was a rookie then," he said, "and I remember I would get jittery in the outfield, and, sure, there were times when I wished they wouldn't hit the ball my way. I don't anymore, though."

Met rookie infielder Wayne Garrett said, "You have to get jittery at times. We all do, I think, when there's pressure. I remember a close game recently when Roberto Clemente was up in the ninth. I was at second base. I knew they were pitching him outside.

"I said to myself, 'That son-of-a-gun's going to hit me one—I just hope it's not too hard.' He did, and it wasn't too hard...."

The players feel that Hodges, because of his placid demeanor (he even argues with umpires with hands behind his back), is greatly responsible for the team not tightening up.

Once, for example, Ken Boswell picked up a batting helmet in front of Hodges in the dugout, on his way to the plate.

"Kenny," said Hodges, "a few of us were talking and we think you were pressing the last time up." Boswell blinked. "And," continued Hodges, "we also think you'll swing better this time." Boswell and Hodges and a few of the other Mets nearby laughed. Tension was eased.

J.C. Martin, the catcher, was with Agee on that rattled White Sox team in 1967 and says the same thing can't happen here. In a recent game, for example, he watched Clendenon drop an easy infield throw. But no runs scored. The Mets won. "It scared me. It reminded me of the White Sox's first game against Washington at the end of the '67 season," Martin said. "Tommy McGraw, as good a fielding first baseman as there is, dropped a throw on the first batter in the first inning. The runner scored and we lost 1–0."

On the field and on the bench, pennant contenders are goosey with expectation as they watch their hitters, their pitchers, and the scoreboard for progress of the other games.

"At the end of an inning," said pitcher Jerry Koosman recently, "I came into the dugout. The dugout is crowded now because of all the new guys up from the minors. I looked around. Then Tom Seaver jumped up. 'Sit here,' he said. 'I'm too nervous to sit, anyway.' I said I was, too. So we both stood. And there was a hole on the bench."

THE NIGHT THE CUBS LOST THE PENNANT TO THE METS

September 30, 1969

(The world knows how New York fans reacted the night the Mets won their division championship. But what Chicago Cub followers did that evening is much less known. Now, after a period of mourning has been duly respected, it can be revealed what one Cub fan went through.)

CHICAGO—HE SLOWLY REACHED OVER and turned off the radio because he did not care to listen to the description of the Mets' championship celebration, of how New York fans poured onto the field of Shea Stadium, of how the champagne poured over the players' heads in the clubhouse.

Barry Holt is a Chicago Cub fan. He has been ever since he was a kid growing up on the North Side, going to games whenever he could and, when he couldn't, playing a form of stickball in the streets and sliding—actually sliding—into the second base manhole cover the way he thought Roy Smalley might have done.

So Barry Holt took the end of the Cubs' phenomenal fade with grace, but with a hand that shook just a bit to be sure, and with a blink that brought the curtain down on a single, slippery tear.

At 31 years old, a lawyer now, a family man, Holt remains a knowledgeable and enthusiastic fan, a "true" Cub fan as the breed was known much, much before a group of raucous beer-and-baseball cranks made such a to-do over being "Bleacher Bums."

Holt gets station KMOX out of St. Louis and he has been listening to Harry Caray describe the Cardinals game against the Mets in New York the last week in September. If the Mets won, they would clinch the Eastern Division championship.

"To the very end," said Holt, "I thought that maybe the impossible was possible. That the Mets could lose to the Cardinals, and then to Philadelphia, and then the Cubs would win all their games and would be two games down with the two games of the season left against the Mets in Chicago.

"I didn't want to turn the radio on until I figured it was about the sixth inning. I mean, I couldn't listen to it if the Mets jumped off to a big lead. So I thought I'd wait and then hope that when I put it on the Cardinals would be ahead."

During the season, Holt said he would "kill" himself to listen to the game on the radio or watch it on television. At one time, he used to "kill" himself to get out to Wrigley Field. Not this year. When once he would watch 70 games or so in person, this year he saw only 20. "It was a different kind of summer out there," said Holt.

A lot of old Cub fans went to fewer games this year because it was so crowded with people who had never been out there before.

"The real Bleacher Bums used to sit in right-center field. They'd do a lot of betting. This year you'd see them out there sometimes, but they'd be scattered. You'd find one sitting quietly between two guys in crash helmets piling up beer cans. It was a less knowledgeable crowd, but tremendously loyal, anyway. But I spent more time listening to the games on the radio than ever before."

He turned on the radio on that late September evening and it happened to be the sixth inning and he heard that a rookie, a Campisi, was pitching for St. Louis.

"Obviously Carlton had been knocked out. But I hoped that he had come up with a sore arm and was taken out. Then Harry Caray told the score, 6–0, and I knew the Cardinals wouldn't touch Gary Gentry.

"But then in the ninth inning the Cardinals got men on second and third with no outs. And I felt like I was watching a horse race and I had money on the horse that ran dead last, but I didn't tear up my ticket because I hoped the tote board would flash that the other 11 horses had been disqualified.

"Then Vada Pinson struck out. And Joe Torre hit a bouncer to Harrelson who threw out to Weis and then to Clendenon for the double play.

"And it was like the old days when you thought Bob Rush would soon realize his potential and be better than Newcombe, and Smalley was better than Marty Marion. Those were the days when you asked someone how the Cubs did, and they said the Cubs lost and you knew the Cubs didn't lose, but that the game ended before they could catch up."

GIL HODGES ISN'T THINKING ABOUT TOMORROW

October 9, 1969

ON THAT DAY OF days, just after the New York Mets had beaten Atlanta for the third time to win the National League pennant, Donn Clendenon floated out of the rain of champagne in the locker room and into his manager's office.

Met first baseman Clendenon, sober as a supplicant and neglecting only to be genuflect, said to Gil Hodges, "You're a genius. Every move you've made has been right."

"Oh, I make mistakes," said Hodges, with a wry smile. "I just don't admit them."

Hodges was, in fact, an unmitigated genius this season, having led the Mets from ninth place last season to the World Series in 1969. But it did not come easy. It took Hodges six previous, second-division seasons to fully grasp the genius business.

Now that he is in it up to his ears, Hodges remains aware of how hazardous and fleeting the occupation of being a genius actually is.

Two days after the pennant celebration, for example, Hodges sat in that same manager's sanctuary and received the intelligence that Joe Gordon, who reputedly had done a fine job as manager of the new Kansas City team, was out of a job.

"You never know, you never know," said Hodges. "Tomorrow might be..." and the words disappeared in a wisp of reflection.

And Hodges could easily have been contemplating the plight of recent pennant-winning managers, all of whom were in the genius business for at least one summer before giving way to a greater genius in another town.

There was Dick Williams of Boston who masterminded another "impossible dream" in 1967. The Red Sox also went from ninth place the year before to become American League champions. He was recently fired.

In 1966, Hank Bauer's brain lurked behind Baltimore's pennant and four-game World Series sweep of Los Angeles. He was bounced before the 1968 season had ended, went to Oakland, and received similar treatment before this season was over.

Sam Mele was the baseball counterpart of Einstein in 1965, as his Minnesota Twins won the American League pennant. By late summer of 1967, he had been evicted from Metropolitan Stadium.

The year before that, Yogi Berra, now one of Hodges' coaches, had his brilliant managerial head lopped off right after, of all things, winning a pennant for the New York Yankees.

"I never think about being fired," said Hodges. "I know it's not out of the realm of possibility. It's like when I was a player. I couldn't worry about being traded, though I knew it was probably inevitable. All you can do is think about doing your best."

In 1963, his first year as a manager, at Washington, the Senators won 60 games. And finished last. They won 62 in 1964, and were ninth. In 1965, they won 70 and finished eighth. The next season they won 71 and, again, were eighth. In 1967, they won 76 and tied Baltimore, the defending world champions, for sixth.

The Mets then sought Hodges, and Washington reluctantly game him up. Promptly, Hodges had a heart attack, which some black humorists considered a sure omen for one's association with the Mets. But Hodges improved the Mets slightly in 1968. They won 73 games, one more than the previous season. Spectacularly, they won 100 games this year.

Hodges said, unnecessarily to be sure, that winning the pennant with the Mets was his greatest thrill as a manager. But his most glorious personal baseball experience, he said, was his first time at bat for Brooklyn in the seventh game of the 1952 World Series. After having gone six games and 19 at-bats without a hit, the popular first baseman received a standing ovation from the sympathetic Ebbets Field crowd. To no avail. He went 0-for-4 and became the only regular in World Series history not to get a hit in seven games.

"I hit a few of them pretty good, but I couldn't seem to hit one safely," he said at the time.

"That just goes to prove I go from one extreme to the other."

And so, knows the level-headed Hodges, has Dick Williams, Hank Bauer, Sam Mele, and Yogi Berra, to name but four other former geniuses.

• • •

The Mets under Gil Hodges finished third in the National League East in 1970 and '71. On April 2, 1972, with the team in spring training, Hodges suffered a heart attack and died, two days short of his 48th birthday. Yogi Berra was named to succeed him.

WILL THE METS INSPIRE UNITY IN NEW YORK?

September 17, 1969

METS DAY IN NEW York. A ticker-tape parade was planned by Mayor Lindsay immediately after "The Amazin's"—as they are known by some, "Destiny's Darlings," as they are known by others—after this team beat the Baltimore Orioles for the baseball championship of the world.

The motorcade burrows under the avalanche of confetti and streamers and here and there a baseball player's hairy, gnarled hand pokes through and waves, like a man buried in a drift.

But is this just an outburst of enthusiasm and appreciation from the local fandom for exciting games won and daring plays done? Not anymore, it isn't. The days are over when gents in bowlers and stiff collars would celebrate their team's victory for the pure pleasure of winning at play.

Now, you read that the Mets have pumped optimism into the lives of the downtrodden, the working stiff; these people, say some social observers, can now grasp a straw of hope from the success of the Mets. The Mets were the ragamuffins of baseball until this sudden season. It is Horatio Alger revisited, but with a bedsheet flapping from the mansion window. The sheet is inscribed and reads: "Macy's Long Island Warehouse Loves the Mets."

So, a city councilman states publicly that the Mets were the power that kept the city peaceful this summer; that is, the town was too busy following the Amazin' Mets to fool around with race riots and the like. (But one skeptic says it was a rainy summer, not a winning summer, that kept the fires from burning.)

Others declaim that the Mets returned to joy to a heretofore joyless city, a city torn by contention in almost every area.

And people are saying that if the Mets can win a championship, then the city could certainly pool its abilities and resources and come up a winner, too.

"We oughta make Hodges the mayor," said a man at a stand selling newspapers. "He took a lousy team and made it terrific. Couldn't he do that with this city?"

The city has certainly been stormed by M-Days lately. Just the day before the fifth and final game of the series, there was Moratorium Day. Many citizens from the entire spectrum of New York humanity participated in peaceful demonstrations opposing the war in Vietnam; others opposed Moratorium Day.

But the Mets were still on a lot of minds. And pamphlets were distributed in front of the ballpark. They had Met pitcher Tom Seaver's name and picture on them and there was a reprint of a newspaper story in which Seaver said he would take out a newspaper ad after the series. The ad would read: "If the Mets can win the Series, the United States can get out of Vietnam." (Seaver, upon learning of these pamphlets, was irked because his name was used without his permission.)

Just a little over two months ago, there was a third M-Day. Moon Day. Another ticker-tape parade cascaded upon three Houston Astro fans who made the first man-landing trip to the moon. Even this wasn't simply a celebration for a successful trip and the return of a collection of pretty rocks. This was not just one small step for man. But it was one giant step for mankind. And people said, "It just goes to prove what we can do if we set our minds to something. Let's fix up the country the way we fixed up that moon shot."

The oldest established continuous M-Day in America is, of course, Mother's Day. President Wilson in 1915 proclaimed it an annual national observance. A lot of people thought then that harmony would come bounding up like a playful lapdog once we remembered officially how much we loved our mothers, especially since most of us have one.

Mother's Day may have helped improve our litters, but not necessarily our lives. And aren't people already forgetting what accomplishment the Moon Men symbolized? And Moratorium Day may just be a dying candle in the night. And so, sadly, the social significance of the Mets' amazin' triumph may have as much historic impact as the come-from-behind "Miracle Boston Braves" of 1914.

But maybe, just maybe, the Mets are, as their outfielder Ron Swoboda said, "The saints of lost causes."

SWEEPING WAVE OF METMANIA HARDLY RIPPLES WALDEN POND

October 10, 1969

AN UNCOMMON ENTHUSIASM HAS swept New York this summer and fall. It is known as Metmania, deriving from the success of a once-hapless baseball team called "The Mets."

Amid a sea of fanaticism in America's most thickly populated metropolis, where thought has been inundated by screams of "We're Number One," it seems appropriate to seek the view of one with a clear perspective. So the spirit of Henry David Thoreau was sought.

Essayist E. B. White recently said, "I doubt if Thoreau would have a particle of interest in the Mets. I think he would view the whole thing with a jaundiced eye."

In 1845, Thoreau left his hometown of Concord, Massachusetts, to live alone alongside the nearby Walden Pond. He did so to "front only the essential factors of life." He wrote of the experience in his classic "Walden," from which came the stuff of the following interview.

It seems to support White's belief.

Mr. Thoreau, living in the woods as you do, I don't suppose you have seen any Mets games. But I imagine you have read about them.

I am sure that I never read any memorable news in a newspaper. If you read of one man robbed, or one house burned, or one vessel wrecked, or one steamboat blown up, or one lot of grasshoppers in the winter—we never need read of another.

Does this mean that if one team overcomes adversity to strive from behind to win a pennant, as did the Boston Braves of 1914 or the New York Giants of 1951 and the Mets of 1969, that that is all we need to know of it?

One is enough. If you are acquainted with the principle, what do you care for the myriad instances and applications?

What the Mets did, though, seemed quite unusual to millions of people. They were 9½ games behind the Cubs on August 13, then rose to win their division championship by eight games. Then they beat the Braves three straight for the National League pennant.

Our life is frittered away by detail. An honest man has hardly need to count more than his 10 fingers, or in extreme cases, he may add his 10 toes, and lump the rest. Simplicity, simplicity, simplicity.

Do you see any joy in baseball, the way a pitcher struggles to pitch to spots, the way runners slide into bases to avoid tags, the way outfielders chase down long fly balls?

It is not necessary that a man should earn his living by the sweat of his brow, unless he sweats easier than I do.

The Mets' television announcer said recently that Mets fans have suffered with poor teams for seven years. Do you think this kind of suffering was unusual?

The mass of men lead lives of quiet desperation. What is called resignation is confirmed desperation. A stereotyped but unconscious despair is concealed even under what are called the games and amusements of mankind.

Well, now there is a great jubilation among the fans. How do you interpret this?

When we are unhurried and wise, we perceive that only great and worthy things have any permanent and absolute existence, that petty fears and petty pleasures are but the shadow of reality. This is exhilarating and sublime...by consenting to be deceived by shows, men establish and confirm their daily life of routine and habit everywhere, which still is built on purely illusory foundations.

Then I suppose you would have gone running onto the Shea Stadium field with the other fans to celebrate the championship victories *(Now, Mr. Thoreau quoted Mencius)*:

"That in which men differ from brute beasts is a thing very inconsiderable: the common herd lose it very soon."

But do you see any social value in the Mets' successes after years of frustration?

If one advances confidently in the direction of his dreams, and endeavors to live the life which he has imagined, he will meet with success unexpected in coming hours.

And what do you usually do during World Series time?

In October I (go) a-graping to the river meadows.

ART SHAMSKY WILL NEVER FORGET HIS WORLD SERIES DEBUT

October 14, 1969

"I'LL REMEMBER IT ALL winter, and I'm sure I'll think about it the rest of my life, that I had a chance to do something very big in front of the whole nation, and to do something very important for my team, for my friends, for my folks—and for me, and I failed," said Art Shamsky.

Shamsky of the New York Mets was recalling his first time at bat in a World Series game.

It was the opening game in Baltimore. The Orioles were ahead 4–1, two were out and two were on for the Mets in the top of the ninth.

And jubilation in the Mets dugout was something less than what it was in Times Square on V-E Day.

"Grab a bat," manager Gil Hodges said softly to Shamsky, and the sound of his voice rumbled through the dugout the way it would have in a tomb. And Shamsky's stomach seemed to be hopping here and there in his abdomen, as it had been for the entire game.

Shamsky was being called now to pinch-hit for relief pitcher Ron Taylor. The 50,000 or so people in Memorial Stadium and the millions watching on television and listening on the radio knew that a home run would tie the game and inject momentum into the Amazin' Mets, a team that now had a foot and a half in the grave.

"A pinch hitter has to feel tight going up there," said Shamsky, "and anyone that says he doesn't is lying. Especially in a World Series. You only have one chance, and so you can't afford to take any pitches. You have to swing at the first good one. And your muscles are stiff from sitting and you're tense from thinking about when you might get the call."

Shamsky has another problem, a minor case of inferiority complex with the bat. "I've never had that much confidence in myself as a hitter. Even this year, when I hit .300 for the first time in my professional career. So I'm always worried that I won't measure up."

At the plate, though, Shamsky has superior powers of concentration. As he stepped into the batter's box, his thoughts of that television camera, with tentacles all across the nation, vanished. It was just him and the pitcher, Mike Cuellar. He swung and missed at the first pitch. He hit the second sharply to the second baseman, who threw Shamsky out. The game was over.

He hit the ball hard, as he was supposed to, and had hoped to. It was all he could do. The ball just did not find a hole. It was hardly the performance of a goat, a failure, an Ernie Lombardi falling asleep at home plate as the winning run slides by, or Mickey Owen dropping a third strike to open a rally for the opposing team, or even Tony Lazzeri striking out with the bases loaded against Grover Cleveland Alexander—all World Series legends of the art of flopping.

"It just seems that my big moments somehow end in failure," said lean, dark-haired Art Shamsky. "I remember my first time at bat in the major leagues. It was 1965. I was with Cincinnati and we were playing in St. Louis, my hometown. My parents were there. I pinch-hit in the ninth inning, against Bob Gibson. Of all people to break in against! I was so scared that my arms felt locked. He struck me out.

"Even in 1966, when I hit four straight homers to tie a major league record, even that ended in failure. We lost both games.

"But you know, we played in Cooperstown once and I saw my bat in the Hall of Fame, the one I hit those four homers with. It was with the bats of the other players who had done the same thing, and I was proud to be with those guys, like Lou Gehrig, who were so much better hitters than me. I'll never forget that experience. But I know I'll never forget my first time up in a World Series, either."

• • •

Art Shamsky, who batted .538, with seven hits in 13 at-bats in the postseason against Atlanta, went hitless in six at-bats in the World Series, which the Mets won in five games. Suffering back problems, Shamsky retired after the 1972 season.

JACKIE ROBINSON AND ED CHARLES, AMONG OTHERS

November 1, 1972

I SHARE SOMETHING WITH former National League pitchers. Jackie Robinson haunts my memory, too.

Days after Robinson's death, I was still thinking of a lunch I had with him about four years ago. I had walked into his midtown Manhattan office to pick him up. He was on the phone, legs up on his desk, talking to some friend about a celebrity golf event in which, this year, he had not been invited. Robinson had gone to several previous tournaments in the series.

He wanted the friend to find out why there was no invitation. Did it have anything to do with some of his recent controversial remarks about "racism in America"? "We'll give it a good fight," Robinson said, smiling. He had the shaft of his glasses in his teeth.

Jackie Robinson, it seemed to me, *enjoyed* the fight. Even then, at age 49, suffering from diabetes, failing eyesight that would render him virtually blind before his death, high blood pressure, heart trouble, the drug addiction of his son, Jackie Jr., he was still combative.

"Look at Jackie now," wrinkled Satchel Paige told me a couple years ago, "and his hair's white and you'd think he was my grandfather."

He didn't sound old, though speaking in that dynamic falsetto he sounded more like Liberace than you'd expect of this rough ex-ballplayer, so menacing on the bases, who suffered so many pitchers trying to stuff baseballs in his ear, who broke the color barrier in a white elitist game and had to live with "black bastard" echoing though the dugouts and the caverns of his mind.

At his funeral, however, the Reverend Jesse Jackson's eulogy rang though the great vaulted Riverside Church, and the phrase for Jackie Robinson had changed from "black bastard" to "black knight."

Robinson had become a Hall of Famer, but his place in history does not stop at Cooperstown. Baseball provided the setting for a milestone in the American human rights struggle. Robinson helped open doors of opportunity not only in sports but in many other areas of America.

Jesse Jackson compared Robinson to Louis Pasteur and Gandhi and Martin Luther King and Jesus as a man who gave others hope by example. This may seem a wild exaggeration. But if you were a 13-year-old black boy like Ed Charles living in Florida—where blacks were still being lynched—it was not so wild.

"I owe so much to Jackie Robinson," said Charles, an ex–major league infielder. "All black players do. We tend to forget. I never will. When Jackie Robinson came through my hometown with the Dodgers in 1947, it was the biggest day of my life. It was the biggest day of all of our lives.

"I realized then I could play in the major leagues. They pushed the old people to the ballpark in wheelchairs and some came on crutches and a few blind people were led to the park.

"When it was over, we chased the Dodger train as far as we could with Robinson waving to us from the back. We ran until we couldn't hear the sound anymore. We were exhausted but we were never so happy."

I told Robinson at lunch that I had recently been in Chicago and had talked casually with a black shoeshine boy in his early teens. I asked who his favorite baseball player was.

"Ernie Banks," the bootblack said. "Willie Mays, too. Yeah, I wanna be a ballplayer, too. Like him."

I asked the fellow if he wanted to be a ballplayer like Jackie Robinson, too? "Who?" he asked.

"Jackie Robinson."

"Never heard of him."

This was neither sad nor surprising to Robinson. He dealt in realities.

"It's true that many black kids have never heard of me," he said. "But they haven't heard of the Montgomery bus boycott in 1956, either. And that was the beginning of Dr. King's nonviolent movement. They don't get any kind of black history in their school books. They want it. They read only about white society. They're made to feel like nonpersons. This is frustrating. It's up to the power structure of this country to understand these kids. Then the burnings, the muggings, the dope, the despair, much of what plagues this country will be greatly lessened.

"Black athletes playing today carry prestige. They can be very significant in explaining the problems and encouraging the kids. But I've been out of baseball for 12 years. The kids look at me like I'm just an old-timer."

The "old-timer" fought until he died. He fought for better housing, he fought for better schooling, he fought for greater say for blacks in government, he fought for a black manager in baseball.

While he angered the mossbacks who thought he wanted too much too fast, he continued to inspire with the courage of his fight that would encompass freedom for all men.

"No grave can hold his body down," said Jesse Jackson. "It belongs to the ages. His spirit is perpetual. And we are all better because a man with a mission passed our way."

• • •

Ed Charles, the oldest Met on the 1969 World Series champions, at age 36, was the team's third baseman. He hit .207 that season, .133 in the Series, and then retired from baseball with an eight-season batting average of .263.

TOM SEAVER LOSES HIS OVERCOAT

February 4, 1970

ROCHESTER, NEW YORK—For an individual to be talented, famous, youthful, facial features all in order, prospering, coordinated, bright, and a New York Met is one thing, but to be humble, too, is a combination as near to impossible as to be sacrilege.

Humility is not necessarily a quality for which one plots down and plods toward, but rather is often thrust by circumstance upon you—like fame.

Humility may not be easy when one is saddled with all of the above adjectives. Yet Tom Seaver gives it a good try, with assistance from various outside forces.

A case in point is a recent safari that took Seaver from the jungle of New York to the frontier outpost of Rochester where he received the $10,000 Hickok belt as professional athlete of 1969.

The trip was made by overnight train, the most humbling experience for him since he decided, as a rookie pitcher in 1967, that since he got Henry Aaron to hit into a double play the first time he ever faced him, the second time would be a snap. The second time: Aaron's home run ball, said Seaver, is probably still ricocheting around the upper deck in Atlanta's stadium.

The train was to leave Sunday night at 10:30. Seaver, being honored as Player of the Year by the New York baseball writers, had to flee their banquet to make the train.

Bob Goodman, an enterprising public relations man, was assigned to make certain Seaver was on that train. Goodman and Seaver made the train, barely. Which is nearly a pun since in the rush Seaver's overcoat disappeared.

Others in the private car included Curt Blefary, lately of the New York Yankees; Joe Louis, the former prize fighter; Murray Goodman, Bob's father and also a public relations man; and several newspapermen.

Louis went immediately to sleep in his berth. The others stayed up, some well into the night, jostled and dreamy as the train crawled through the black-bandaged night, to steal a Welsh poet's phrase.

Somehow the talk got around to the greatest athlete you'd ever seen, the greatest athletic feat, and a few other silly, insoluble, wholly disputable and utterly absorbing topics.

No one could really decide just what the greatest athlete should do—just one sport, or the decathlon like Bill Toomey? But names such as Jim Brown, Oscar Robertson, Clay/Ali, and a surprise, Doug Atkins, were mentioned. Blefary said Mickey Mantle, his boyhood idol.

Seaver said, well, probably Sandy Koufax. As for greatest athletic feat, Seaver said for him it was Koufax's four career no-hitters.

Someone else wanted to know if near most-greatest athletic feats counted. If so, he would pick Seaver's almost-perfect game against the Cubs, when a ninth-inning single spoiled it all. Seaver smiled, an expression very different from the one on his face that moment that summer night in Shea Stadium.

Around 2:00 in the morning, Seaver and a newspaperman called it a night and inched into an upper and lower berth compartment that was not made for even taking off one's shoes. The two bumped around like Laurel and Hardy. "Now I know what Rube Walker meant," said Seaver, referring to the Mets' pitching coach, "when he said you really came to know your roommate when teams used to travel by train."

After a few hours of sleep as placid as rolling off Niagara Falls in a barrel, the call to arise resounded over the clack on the track. Seaver arose, cheery as a weathered tombstone.

Outside it was raining in the dark before dawn and Seaver and the others waited for the chartered bus with the bad memory. Blefary gave Seaver his coat, to keep the shoulder warm.

And there for all time, etched in memory like a daguerreotype, was Tom Seaver in the dark and chill-rain, and thinking that tomorrow morning he must again be up at 6:00 to catch a plane. His wife, Nance, expected him back early to their new home is Greenwich, Connecticut. He was to finish painting the pantry.

• • •

In 1969, Tom Seaver led the major leagues with 25 wins (against seven losses), had a 2.21 earned-run average, and, after having been the losing pitcher in Game 1 of the World Series, beat the Orioles 2–1 in 10 innings to win Game 4.

THE SAINTS OF LOST CAUSES

May 22, 1989

TWENTY YEARS LATER THEY were different, of course, grayer, rounder at the belt, and with noticeably less spring in their step. No longer did they appear, as one of them, Ron Swoboda, the outfielder, said back then, like "the saints of lost causes."

On Saturday at Shea Stadium, the 20th reunion was held of the 1969 world champion New York Mets, "The Amazin's," as some called them, or even "Destiny's Darlings."

They won the title in only their eighth season as a franchise, a franchise that in its early years was a national joke, a team so upside down that their first manager, Charles Dillon Stengel, once turned in the dugout and asked, "Can't anybody here play this game?" and for whom, as a sportswriter named Dick Young noted, "a superstar was someone who could put on his baseball shoe without spiking himself."

In the previous year, 1968, they finished ninth, and before that, 10th, ninth, 10th, 10th, 10th, and 10th.

But the 1969 Mets turned out differently, led by a young, broad-shouldered, bright, laughing, and hard-throwing pitcher from Fresno, California, named Tom Seaver, also known as Tom Terrific....

They beat the Braves in three straight games, and the Orioles in five games, for the championship. Ron Swoboda, that elephantine outfielder, momentarily turned into a swan and made a diving catch in right field that would forever be the envy of saints of lost causes. And the team's greatest hero, Seaver, would lose the opening game of the Series, and win the fourth, but could keep things in perspective afterward. "Well," he said, "I'm the only pitcher in Mets history to lose a World Series game."...

What happened to the Amazin' Mets? A few years afterward Hodges collapsed and died of a heart attack. Donn Clendenon, the first baseman and most valuable player in the World Series, became a lawyer in South Dakota, but also became a drug addict. He remains a lawyer, and says he has kicked the cocaine habit.

Jerry Grote, the catcher, is a real estate salesman; Swoboda is a sports broadcaster in New Orleans; Seaver announces ballgames for the Yankees and for national games on NBC; Ron Taylor, the relief pitcher, is team physician for the Toronto Blue Jays; Nolan Ryan still throws fastballs for a living; and Art Shamsky owns a restaurant, Legends, near City Hall, where, 20 years earlier, he and his teammates were showered with confetti in a victory ticker-tape parade.

It was a joyous time, a thrilling time, but, in the light of history, not necessarily a meaningful time. The Amazin' Mets winning the World Series meant no more and no less on the world stage than the Miracle Boston Braves of 1914, who went from last place in July to sweep the powerful Philadelphia A's in the World Series.

The Braves couldn't keep us out of World War I. And the Mets couldn't get us out of Vietnam. For that matter, though, neither could the men on the moon.

II.

FROM YOGI TO MOOKIE, AND BEYOND

LEO DUROCHER DOESN'T READ NEWSPAPERS?

June 1, 1970

"ABOUT SIX MONTHS AGO," said Leo Durocher (who perhaps is not the best source for this information), "I quit reading the sports pages. I got tired reading fiction."

The Chicago Cubs' manager sat with feet upon his desk in the visitors' clubhouse at Shea Stadium and cracked a wry smile at his remark.

He is speaking to the press now, a reversal from last season. Then he cut off communications with the news media, except for his own pregame and postgame radio shows, when his stratagems and the servings of his pitchers began to be hit hard. The Cubs fell from an 8½ -game lead in the National League's Western Division to a second-place finish, eight games behind the New York Mets.

He was now telling of a time several years ago when he managed the New York Giants and had said a similar thing, that he was not reading the sports pages.

"One writer was knockin' my brains out every day," he recalled. "I felt like killing him. But another writer gave me some advice on how to handle this guy, and I took it.

"After every game, this guy who was knockin' my brains out came into my office and I answered all his questions with a smile.

"After about 10 days, he said to me, 'Leo, how come you're being so nice to me, what with the way I've been knockin' your brains out?' And I said, 'Oh, really? Gee pal, I haven't been reading your stuff.' That really got him. He wrote beautiful stuff about me after that."

If it is true that Durocher has not been reading sports sections for six months, then he did not read that *Look Magazine* piece in March which was called "How Durocher Blew the Pennant." In it, he was called "the most unprincipled man in sports."

"Naw, I didn't read it," he said. "But a lot of my friends told me what was in it. A lot of guys write things about me and I never see 'em. I wouldn't know 'em if I tripped over 'em. But this guy who wrote it [William Barry Furlong], they tell me's got buck teeth and dirty fingernails. You gotta hate this guy right away. Right? I mean, buck teeth and dirty fingernails."

What, then, are Durocher's reading habits, now?

"I read everything except the sports pages," he said. "Like the *Chicago Tribune*, it comes in sections. I get the paper and dump the sports section in the waste basket.

"It reminds me of Mr. Stoneham [Horace Stoneham owns the San Francisco Giants]. Jimmy Powers used to cut Mr. Stoneham's throat every day in a New York paper. So Mr. Stoneham had his secretary cut out Powers' column and drop it into the waste basket and then put the paper on his desk.

"Most people read the sports for relaxation, to get away from world events. Me, I do the opposite."

Durocher then asked about the article in the recent *Look* by Jim Bouton. "I saw a story in the paper about it with pictures of Mickey [Mantle], Whitey [Ford], and Ralph [Houk]," he said. "Bouton gave it to 'em pretty good. Now why would he do something like that? How much could he have gotten for it? Five thousand dollars maybe. Did he need the money? I could understand it if his kids and wife were starving..."

He was asked what he was doing reading the sports section.

"It was on my desk, turned right to the page, when I came in. I couldn't help see it," he said.

Then he told another story, which he considered humorous, about a sportswriter who had obviously been tippling and staggered into Durocher's office in Chicago last year. The sportswriter asked Durocher if he could do him a favor. Durocher said yes. The guy wanted to borrow money, and Durocher reached into his pocket. (Durocher, ethically, did not mention the amount.)

"The next day, the guy knocks my brains out," said Durocher. "That's not so bad—if he also drops my money on my desk. But I never saw him again."

How did Durocher know the sportswriter slammed him, since he no longer reads the sports section?

"I got friends who told me," he replied.

KRANEPOOL MAKES A COMEBACK AT 26

June 18, 1971

ED KRANEPOOL WILL ALWAYS be an Original Met, which is not the primary reason his name was left off the All-Star computer ballot.

Few of last season's .170 hitters were on the ballot, in fact. Besides, a "Kranepool" to some is indistinguishable from a "Throneberry," say. Who'd have thought, last winter when the ballots were drawn up, that in June Kranepool would be running in the Top 10 circles with a Willie Mays?

It has seemed unlikely ever since Edward Emil Kranepool came up to the major leagues in 1962, a 17-year-old first baseman, blue-eyed, buffalo-big. Soon, a banner appeared in the stands that would flap over Kranepool's head for the rest of his career: "Is Kranepool Over the Hill?" Kranepool still can't laugh about it. ("I feel sorry for those people who have nothing else to do with their lives except write signs," he said.)

Last season, finally, at age 25, the Mets sent Kranepool over the hill. They sent him to the minor leagues, Tidewater. It was late June and Kranepool, in his ninth major league season, had batted just 47 times and turned into an ambulatory damp log.

"I wasn't playing and I wasn't helping myself or the team, and I became introverted. I didn't want to talk to anybody and I didn't want anybody to talk to me," he said.

"The easiest thing then would have to be to quit. But I still thought I could play. I didn't want to run and hide. I didn't want to go out when I was on the bottom. A lot of guys go down and stay down. I was determined to play myself back into the big leagues.

"I was told on the road that I was being sent down. I didn't see any of my teammates before I left. One day you're in—the next day you're gone. There's no time for tears.

"But the pressure was on. I mean, I knew that I had three months of my baseball career left, if I didn't hit. I batted in 45 runs in five weeks at Tidewater. I must've been doing something right. It was so hot, so depressing in the bushes. You had to play hard or give up."

This spring he felt he would be traded, and the transformation of enthusiasm and energy that gripped him in the minor leagues carried over. He said he was actually playing, not for Met manager Gil Hodges, but for the other 23 managers. "That's why I really busted my butt," he said. "I wanted them to see me and trade for me."

Hodges liked what he saw enough to hang on to Kranepool. Not so Ron Swoboda, Kranepool's friend and business partner. (They recently opened a restaurant in a New York suburb.) Swoboda wanted to be traded from the Mets, and was. He is with the Expos now.

"And not playing," said Kranepool. "He's away from home and sitting. If he was going to sit, he might as well have been sitting here. He's worse off now than before."

And Kranepool is riding a tide. In fact, the *New York Daily News* has campaigned for All-Star write-in votes for Kranepool.

"It's ego-satisfying to get this attention now," said Kranepool. "Maybe I have an outside chance. But I couldn't beat out McCovey for first base. He's probably the best in the game at that position. And Cepeda will get a lot of votes. So will Donn [Clendenon, with whom Kranepool platoons]."

In 1965, Kranepool was named to the All-Star team but did not get into the game. But he doesn't kid himself about being a star.

"I'm struggling all the time," he said. "Most of us are struggling all the time. The game is very difficult, unless you're a superstar. Look at Shamsky now. He batted .300 last season. Now he's below .200. And he's depressed because he's not playing. Not much to cheer about.

"I know how Artie's stomach is churning. A superstar doesn't know what he's going through, but I do."

WILLIE MAYS AT TWILIGHT

March 21, 1973

ST. PETERSBURG, FLORIDA—WILLIE MAYS and his small shadow at his heels created a flurry of activity at home plate. This was the first inning and Mays' first appearance in a spring training game this year. There was a polite—and what may be assumed hopeful—round of applause here at Al Lang Field. The stands were filled with folks from this retirement community who appreciate an old fellow's effort.

Mays and his shadow, which was slightly in the early afternoon sun, each acknowledged the reception with a characteristically quick wiggle of the bat.

It was a sultry day. The palm trees behind the outfield fence were still. A clump of dust kicked up by Dodger pitcher Claude Osteen rose heavily. One's shirt grew moist from the exertion of just *standing* in the sun.

Mays will be 42 years old on May 6. He has played 21 major league seasons, and his terrific career is either over or has one more year, depending, says Mays, on how he swings the bat in spring training.

Right now, he looked lively and light at the plate. His helmet was fastened tight on his head. His knit, concentrating brows, puckered lips, and soft Mets cap stuffed in his left back pocket gave the impression that he was still the ebullient "Say Hey" kid of Polo Grounds lore.

The eye deceives. Mays is an aging veteran hanging on. His knees have been mean to him. They must be constantly drained of fluid. And though he holds so many baseball records (only man to twice hit 30 homers and steel 30 bases in a season, 6,992 outfield putouts—which gave a hint at his versatility) and is a certain Hall of Famer, he seems peevish in his familiar squeaky voice and oversensitive about his declining abilities. He has some reason, however.

He has a manager who, for the first time in his career, would rather Mays got lost. It is difficult, though, to fault Met manager Yogi Berra if you are pragmatic—easier if you are romantic.

Berra and Mays appear to be two men who respect each other but know that the town—the team—isn't big enough for the both of them. They have had two confrontations already this spring. On the first day of spring training Mays showed up late. Berra said practice begins at 10:00 AM. Mays said he knows how to train, what his body requires, that he's always in shape, anyway. Berra said all 25 men on his squad get equal treatment, that Mays may exclude exercises but he must be in uniform.

Second clash came out Saturday when Mays did not show up at all. He turned up in Arizona, visiting his wife. He was fined $1,000 by Berra. Mays admitted he was wrong in not telling the manager where he was going.

Besides having to deal with a separate set of standards for Mays, Berra must also handle ghostly realities. Mays is not the player he used to be ("If I said I was, I'd be fooling nobody, including myself," admits Mays), and Berra believes that one of his younger players could be the center fielder all season. But Mays is trying to prove to himself and Berra that at 42 he is still better than guys 22.

Berra knows that if Mays wants to play one more season, he must be carried on the club. Mays was bought from San Francisco last spring by Mets owner Joan Payson, a great fan of Mays'. Berra had no say in the deal. But if Mays does stay, Berra must carry a "caddy"—a veteran to take over in late innings—

for Mays, and will not be able to keep one promising youngster on the roster.

Mays' recent history is that he does well at the beginning of the season, but fades in the hot summer.

Last season, for example, after dramatically winning games with home runs in his first appearance as a Met in Shea Stadium and in Candlestick Park, he played only a handful of games after the July All-Star break because of faulty knees.

Before the game here, Mays saw Dodger manager Walt Alston. "You going to play this season?" asked Alston lightly. Just as lightly, Mays retorted, "How come everybody's trying to get me to quit?" There was a serious undertone.

In his first at-bat, Mays took one ball from Osteen, then slammed a high, inside fastball against the left-field fence. It lit up the ballpark. Glee shot out of the old stands as Willie ended up at second, losing his batting helmet, of course, on his still-quick, dust-puffing, pigeon-toed route.

"That screws Yogi up pretty good," observed a baseball writer for a New York paper, in the press box. "Yogi was hoping Mays would show himself up."

As Mays called time out to retrieve his helmet, one could see with binoculars that his hair is thinning in front and that there are sprigs of gray in his sideburns.

But his body is still powerful and very well-kept, except for his hands, which he says always blister and bleed in spring training, and those well-worn knee hinges.

One also remembered an earlier conversation in which Mays said how lucky he was to be cheered wherever he goes; he said he would be hurt most if he were cheered for what he had been and not for what he can do today. He felt that would be cheating the fans and he would get out of baseball rather than allow that to happen.

On Mays' next time up in his first spring training game, he worked the count to 3-and-2 and then he and his shadow took a mighty swing at an outside-corner curve. "Whooo," went the crowd. But Mays' effort was fruitless. He struck out.

He walked back to the bench; his shadow trailed behind. The shadow was longer than before. The sun was lower. It was later in the afternoon.

• • •

Willie Mays batted .211 in 1973 and retired from baseball, at age 42. He was inducted into the National Baseball Hall of Fame in 1979.

YOGI AND IKE

March 14, 1974

YOGI BERRA IN SOME ways symbolizes an era past (note the television commercial in which he laments his sons' long hair) but in other ways he may be a harbinger.

Yogi Berra last season skillfully managed a physically battered New York Mets team to the National League championship and to within one game of being world champions.

His leadership was calm, unobtrusive, patient, self-effacing, and very much like that of the president of the United States, Dwight Eisenhower, when Yogi was in his heyday as a player with the Yankees.

Yogi appears to be the Ike of baseball. He comes at a time when nostalgia for the '50s is rampant in song and plays and collectibles. It seems a reaction from the violent, war-worn '60s.

Baseball is booming. For the first time, more people watched a single World Series game on TV than viewed the Super Bowl. Also, in some cases the Prussian authoritarianism of Vince Lombardi–type leaders is going the way of the goony bird.

In the '50s, Eisenhower ran the country so that it kind of ran itself as Ike tinkled golf balls into a glass on the rug in the Oval Room. Domestic problems? Foreign entanglements? Oh, things will work themselves out. Clink.

During the 1973 pennant run, pitcher Tom Seaver said Yogi never panicked. "We're doin' the best wit' what we got," said Yogi.

There is a basic likableness in Yogi, just as there was in Uncle Ike, a seeming lack of deviousness. Both even earned endearing nicknames. And each had a sense of the rightness of things:

When Mike Andrews (preciously humiliated by A's owner Charles O. Finley, who put him on the disabled list for making two crucial errors in the second game of the World Series) pinch-hit in the fourth game, Berra stood up and applauded the sympathetic opponent.

When a public school in Little Rock refused to follow court integration orders, Ike called in National Guard troops to carry out the law.

Both Berra and Ike showed narrow concentration in the pursuit of pleasure. Yogi's passion is sandwiches. After a game he would stroll by the sandwich table in the clubhouse, his eyes glazed and scratching his underarms in gustatory anticipation.

Eisenhower's passion was golf. Once, on a desert course in Palm Springs, California, he felt a mad thrum of his kidneys. He dare not halt his game and take relief in the clubhouse, thereby risking the loss of his groove. And since there were no trees or bushes, he summoned his Secret Service retinue and had them form an inverted huddle around him.

Nuance of language was not the forte of either Yogi or Ike. Both had a charming predilection for obfuscation. At one point in his placid presidency, Ike said, "Things are more like they are now than they ever were before."

Just before the fifth game of the World Series, a phone rang in the Met dugout in Shea Stadium. Berra answered in his soft, rumbly voice.

"Yeah? Naw, dear. Can't now, dear. Sure, after the game. Bye, dear." Yogi was asked who the caller was. "Bill White," he replied. "He wanted me to do a radio interview." "You call Bill White 'dear'?" "I mean," he said shyly, "it was Bill White's secretary."

So, it is not impossible to believe that when someone once asked Berra if the Yoo-hoo chocolate drink (he is vice-president of the company) is hyphenated, he is supposed to have said, "Naw, and it's not carbonated, either."

It is also true that Eisenhower, like Yogi, preferred western literature above all other tomes. Ike liked Zane Grey in softcover books. He did not like Zane Grey in hardcover books because they would poke his side when he fell asleep in bed reading one.

Berra went for western belles-lettres in even softer covers, comic books. "In the old days," said Berra, "when we took trains on road trips, I'd stop at the newsstand and buy 10 comics. And most of the guys, like Rizzuto and Lindell, would want to read 'em after me.

"I liked the westerns best, and I liked the guy who used to burn himself up. What's his name? I thought Buck Rogers was great, too. 'Member people used to say that that stuff wouldn't never come true? It did." Berra, however, says he no longer reads comic books. "How come," he was asked. "Taste matured?" "Naw," he said, "they just don't make 'em as good as they used to."

• • •

Yogi Berra was replaced as manager of the Mets in 1975.

PETE ROSE AND TY COBB

March 20, 1974

"A PETE ROSE BY another name still stinks," scribbled one neo-Shakespearean paraphrast on a banner last October here in Shea Stadium.

This literary brainstorm was conceived after Pete Rose of the Cincinnati Reds slammed into Bud Harrelson of the Mets while trying to break up a double play. Dust, spikes, and a fist or two flew.

When Rose returned to his left-field position, after the nefarious inning, boos and whizzing beer bottles greeted him.

Nothing new for Rose. Bleacher Bums in Wrigley Field pelt him with paper clips. Fans in San Francisco bathe him with invective. Even hometown Cincinnati fans, as well as some players, figuratively hold their nose when they hear the name Rose.

He is called hot dog for his headfirst slides, his rifling the ball into the infield after a meaningless out, his executioner-like motion after catching a fly ball, his running, running, even on walks. He has been called, not always with admiration, "Charley Hustle."

"Well," says Rose, "nobody liked Ty Cobb either."

Rose sees himself in the mold of a modern-day Ty Cobb. Rose is a man who hits for average. Last season he batted .338, to win his third league hitting title, and it was his ninth straight season hitting over .300.

The similarities between Rose and Cobb are interesting, both in playing skills and attitude, but the differences are even more absorbing. They differ mainly in degree.

Cobb had a lifetime batting average of .367 for 24 seasons. Rose, going into his 12th big-league year, has a .312 career average.

"Cobb was a super hitter," said Lew Fonseca, the American League batting champion in 1929 and currently a sometime hitting coach with the Cincinnati Reds, "and Pete is a fine hitter.

"I think overall Cobb was more talented, but both showed tremendous desire and used their skills to the ultimate.

"Pete is always asking me about Cobb. I remember his first question. 'Tell me, Lew, was Cobb as tough as they say?'

"'Tougher,' I told him."

Cobb was always getting in brawls, with teammates, with opponents, and with fans, who he would climb into the stands to wound.

"Cobb would do anything to win," said Fonseca. "I remember a story concerning Howard Ehmke, the pitcher. He had pitched at Detroit when Cobb was the playing-manager. Then he was traded to Philadelphia. The first game Ehmke was in against Detroit, [Cobb] hit Ehmke with a pitch. And Ehmke called to Cobb, 'I hit 20 batters for you last year. Now I got one for myself.'"

Cobb would snarl at the opposition, said Fonseca. And, in his way, so does Rose. "One pitcher got Pete out three straight times," said Fonseca. "The fourth time up, Pete shouted to him 'Go down to the bullpen and get warmed up, you ain't got nothin'.'"

One major difference is that Cobb often did not even speak to teammates. Rose talks, though sometimes double-edged. When Rose says to Tony Perez, who passes him in the locker room, "When you gonna knock me in? I'm tired of standin' on second base," it draws a laugh from Perez. And a slow smile from Rose.

Cobb, particularly, was obsessed with being tops. Once, he was angered when he returned to his hotel room and saw his roommate in the bathtub. Cobb screamed, "Get out of there—I'm always first!"

Rose has his peculiarities, too. Once he was giving a baseball clinic for kids on a Hamilton, Ohio, sandlot field, and he let a grounder go through his legs. One kid laughed. Rose skewered him with a look and said, "I make seven errors a season. I have six left."

Both Rose and Cobb were influenced by their fathers. Rose's father taught him to switch-hit ("And I'll always do it, I promised Dad that"), emphasized to young Pete how Enos Slaughter always hustled everywhere on the field.

He told Pete, "That stuff about it's not whether you win or lose, but how you play the game, that's a lot of bunk. If you don't win, you haven't accomplished anything."

"If my father were alive," said Rose, "he'd have bawled me out if I hadn't put the slug on Harrelson."

In his autobiography, written with Al Stump, Cobb talks about the tragedy of his father's death. "My father had his head blown off with a shotgun when I was 18 years old...I've never gotten over it."

It seems that Cobb tried ever after to vindicate his father and produced, in Stump's words, "the most violent, successful, thoroughly maladjusted personality ever to pass across American sports."

As Cobb himself put it, "I had to fight all my life to survive. They were all against me...but I beat the bastards and left them in the ditch."

SEAVER DERAILS THE BIG TRAIN

September 26, 1975

MANNY SANGUILLEN SWUNG AND missed at the third strike, the Shea Stadium scoreboard instantly flashed the news of this historic strikeout, the crowd of 52,410 rose to its feet in the night and cheered, and Tom Seaver, on the mound, suppressed a sigh of relief at the odd turn of events of this season and simply let himself be washed over with the emotion of the moment.

These same fans, though, booed Seaver last season. For after six straight years of nearly unlimited success with the New York Mets, Seaver last season fell to a mediocre record of 11 wins and 11 losses.

He was suffering from an injury that might have ended his career.

However, he managed in the last game of the 1974 season to salvage 201 strikeouts for the year. Sanguillen's strikeout now was Seaver's 200th this season, the eighth straight year he has reached that figure. It broke the ancient record held by a pair of pitching icons, Walter (Big Train) Johnson and Rube Waddell.

As Seaver stood on the mound with a smudge of dirt on the right knee of his white, knickered uniform—dirt accumulated from dragging his leg in delivery—it seemed much of the little-boy love of baseball that Seaver has so exemplified had returned.

He had been aware of the approaching record. "I used to read a lot of baseball books growing up in California," the 30-year-old right-hander would say later, "and I'd read about Walter Johnson and Rube Waddell. And my god! To break their record, well, that's not supposed to happen to me—to me or anyone else. When I was a kid, I didn't dream of playing in the major leagues. It seemed too distant to even dream about."

Seaver is thickly built, with a little fleshiness under his chin. But his brown eyes can light up like a kid's, and his laugh is a kind of cackle.

He remembers faking sickness as a boy and staying home to watch World Series games. When the Pirates dramatically won the 1960 World Series, Tom got so excited he ran into the streets in his pajamas.

He had said that to be good at almost anything, you had to retain a boy's enthusiasm. "I don't believe baseball is any more or less a kid's game than, say, business," he had said. "When we win a big game, we jump around in the clubhouse. When an executive pulls a big deal, he's just as happy. The only difference is that he doesn't jump up and down in his office in his jock strap."

But Seaver on the mound now, hearing those cheers, was every inch a man. He had paid his dues. For example, warming up before his first professional game in the minor leagues, he was so nervous he vomited in the bullpen. At another point, in Toronto, he was belted out of a game, and then went under the stands, kicked some bottles, and cried.

And last season, his fastball had lost its zip; his control of pitches grew shaky.

"It was like a big puzzle, to find out the trouble," he said. "My whole delivery was off. It was frustrating, and awful.

"I guess my sense of manhood, or ego, took some lumps, too. One sets a standard of excellence for himself, then doesn't live up to it after he had lived up to it for a number of years—well, boom, the bottom drops out.

"But I didn't think I was a Steve Blass or a Denny McLain, who suddenly lost it in his prime. I still thought positive about my baseball career. My reflexes were still good, and I still felt strong."

Someone suggested he again see Dr. James Parkes, an osteopath who had treated his pelvic problems in the past. Seaver was now suffering pain in his left hip from a sciatic nerve. The doctor checked him over, then gave a sharp twist to Seaver's hip, and said, you're okay now. "That's all?" asked Seaver. He was incredulous. Still is, for the doctor was right.

His pelvis had been turned out of joint, creating muscle spasms and putting a strain on his right side, which caused his right arm to lower in his pitching delivery.

During spring training this year he worked hard but cautiously. "I didn't want to become another Dizzy Dean. He tried to hurry along after an injury. It ruined his career," said Seaver.

Seaver is a 20-game winner again. And he may win his third Cy Young Award, symbol of the league's best pitcher. The only other three-time winner is Sandy Koufax, who Seaver watched with admiration in the bleachers while in college.

As Seaver stood on the mound after striking out Sanguillen he knew that if he won this game (and he did), it would be his 166th career win, one more than Koufax.

"And then," said Seaver, "I told myself, forget the past, forget the future, and just stand quiet and soak in the cheers."

MISANTHROPE AS CATALYST

May 22, 1982

ANOTHER ONE OF KINGMAN'S Comets was spotted passing through the Flushing sky. It appeared on Wednesday night about 8:00, and it scored three runs.

What was seen was not celestial, of course; it was a baseball, a soaring home run hit by Dave Kingman. It came in the first inning off Tom Seaver and provided the margin of victory in the Mets' 4–2 triumph over the Reds.

And the Shea Stadium fans who had sometimes booed him and chanted "King Phooey" now cheered so lustily that he waved his cap. It was some sight: Kingman, with a reputation for misanthropy, smiling.

So the Mets closed out their latest home stand the way they began their opening one on April 13, when they beat the Phillies, 5–2, with Kingman crashing a three-run homer and waving his cap to the stomping throng.

Overall in this young season, Kingman has 13 home runs, to lead the major leagues, and he has driven in 35 runs, second in the National League. Long and lank at 6'6" and 210 pounds, Kingman, a right-handed hitter, crouches slightly at the plate—pointed elbows and knees—and holds a long bat up and slightly away. The whole picture is one of sharp angles, as if put together with Tinker Toys. And in the air there is a feeling that something exciting may happen.

At Shea Stadium these days a ballgame is as much fun as a picnic, while at Yankee Stadium it's like a last meal. The Mets are playing lively baseball—winning more than expected—and delighting the fans. Oddly the catalyst, Kingman is one who in his time has been deeply sullen and has created turmoil that only a current Yankee could appreciate.

Along with his 305 career home runs, eighth-best among active players, there have been 1,285 strikeouts. In terms of a times-at-bat ratio, he is the second-easiest man in history to strike out. Kingman also may have set some kind of record for creating ill will.

He is 33 years old and has been in the major leagues for 11 seasons. In that time, he has played for six teams—the Mets twice—and he played for four teams in one year, 1977, tying a major league record.

He seemed then the quintessential mercenary in a game in which some fans, in their cozy dream world, put a premium on team loyalty. "I'm just a piece of meat," he once said. "When I can't play anymore, I become disposable to the owners."

True, but his sullenness when unhappy with contract negotiations appeared to extend to his playing. And his petulant swings at curveballs, his lack of concentration at the plate and in the field—at first base, he is the Mets' Dr. Strangeglove—encouraged throaty disapproval from fans.

With teammates, he has sometimes been distant. "Dave has the personality of a tree trunk," a teammate once said. "He's not a bad guy, but if you try to talk to him, about all he does is grunt."

When criticized by the press, Kingman has sometimes reacted by withdrawing. Once, for sport, he dumped a bucket of ice water over the head of a baseball writer.

At times, it seems a new Kingman is trying to emerge from his self-constructed shell. When he rejoined the Mets in 1981, he arrived in spring training with chrome fountain pens, passing them out to reporters in lieu of olive branches.

And this year, with a new manager and a new coaching staff, he has been the model of a team man. He has caught the warm-ups of the batting-practice pitcher, has thrown batting practice, and helps the coaches hit infield fungoes.

"A guy in his position doesn't have to do stuff like that," said manager George Bamberger, in appreciation.

On the playing field, he is comporting himself as if he genuinely cares. He is earning his $750,000-a-year salary with alertness at the plate: besides his long hits, he has laid down some good bunts in needed situations, and on occasion goes wisely with the pitch to right field instead of trying stubbornly to pull every pitch to left. On the bases, he has risked himself for the benefit of the team, sliding headfirst into second and bowling over a catcher to score. On defense—well, he does get dirty.

Kingman has said that the pressure of playing in the big leagues "can drive you up a wall." It is not simply trying to succeed on the playing field but also handling the elements surrounding a major league player. And in 11 seasons it seems he has still not adjusted to it.

He attempts to be a private man in a glaringly public life. "Some players are interested in public relations, but I'm not," Kingman said recently. "I want to be judged by what I do on the field. That's all I care about."

In his year back in New York, he has, for the most part, got his wish from the press. Recently, though, Kingman threw obscenities at a female reporter in the Mets' clubhouse. She was not interviewing him—had never, in fact, interviewed him—and was not standing near him. The attack was seemingly unprovoked. The Mets officially apologized to the writer and her newspaper, though Kingman never did.

"It stunned us," said one of the Mets players, "and it embarrassed the team." Not excusing it, Frank Cashen, the general manager, said that "some people just march to a different drummer." Kingman this season has been the paragon of a ballplayer working at his craft on the field, and if he wishes to be judged only in that regard, he will get no argument from most people.

But if he wants them to keep their distance from him, he ought to do the same. "It's too bad that Dave can't be enjoying this more," said a Met teammate. "He's in his prime, hitting great, and on top of the world. But he always seems to be looking over his shoulder for someone to come up behind him."

Kingman and his peculiar muse have baffled many. However, a sign on the wall in his locker cubicle at Shea Stadium gives an indication of what he sometimes thinks. The sign reads: "I'd rather be fishing."

• • •

Dave Kingman was released by the Mets following the 1983 season.

MIKE MARSHALL, 38, STILL ON A MISSION

August 27, 1981

THE GATE OF THE tall, green bullpen fence in right field in Shea Stadium swung open, and Mike Marshall appeared. Marshall, the Mets' 38-year-old relief pitcher, took one skipping step, like a boy on a lark, and then trotted forthrightly across the outfield to the mound, like a man on a mission.

Called on in the top of the eighth inning in a 1–1 game against Houston Tuesday night, Marshall was the master craftsman. He is stout-chested, with a trim waist and a determined dimple chin. His pitching motion is short, compact, polished, and as spare as a sentence by Hemingway. Marshall pitched two perfect innings and, riding on Mookie Wilson's homer in the home half of the inning, got the victory, his first in more than a year.

Looking back, an observer might find that one little skip out of the bullpen significant. Marshall was apparently happy, having recently returned to baseball after more than a year away, exiled because of his player-union activities, he says; and he was coming out of the bullpen at the point of the game he relishes—under pressure.

The skip also seemed to provide a physical propulsion—especially fitting in the case of Marshall. He holds a Ph.D. in kinesiology—the study of body movement—and has taught it at Michigan State and, in the past year, at St. Cloud State in Minnesota.

The Houston game was Marshall's fifth outing since signing with the Mets last week, and his best. It was reminiscent of the finest days of his 14-year major league career—such as 1974 when he became the first relief pitcher to win the Cy Young Award, and other years in which he set records for innings pitched and games appeared in and saves.

"I wanted to see if Mike could still do it physically," said the Mets' manager, Joe Torre, of the four-day tryout he gave Marshall two weeks ago. "It's obvious he had it. Mike throws a good screwball and a good slider. Anybody with pitches that go two ways is tough. Plus, he knows how to win—he's proved that."

Nothing was said of his union work before he signed on August 19. "I know Mike has a tag by management, but so what, I had one myself," said Torre. "I was the National League player representative and, when I was, Mike was my alternate."

Marshall has always been one of the more outspoken players in regard to players' rights and, according to Marvin Miller, the Major League Players Association executive director, Marshall had been one of the most valuable assets.

"What I did with the Players Association cost me all or parts of six seasons," Marshall says. He says, for example, that his role as American League player representative was one of the reasons the Twins dropped him in June, 1980, and that no other team gave him a chance until the Mets called a couple of weeks ago.

"I had established the American League record for appearing in most games by a pitcher—90—the season before the Twins let me go, and I'd led the league in saves with 32," Marshall says. "Now, I did have some problems early in 1980, but in the last 11⅓ innings before they released me, I had given up just one run. You'd have thought the Twins or someone else would have given more of an opportunity to someone with my record."

Calvin Griffith, president of the Twins, took this position yesterday: "There is no truth that we released Marshall because he was a player representative. We released him because he couldn't get anybody out. His earned-run average was over 6.00."

Before joining the Twins, in 1978, as a free agent, Marshall says he had been told by manager Gene Mauch, "these people aren't very big on player reps."

Nothing new to Marshall. "I'm afraid Mike's problem," wrote Jim Bouton in *Ball Four*, "is that he's too intelligent and has too much education. It's like the Army. When a sergeant found out that a private had been to college, he immediately assumed he couldn't be a good soldier. Right away it was 'There's your college boy for you,' and 'I wonder what our genius has to say about that?' This is the kind of remark they'd make about Marshall."

Marshall has always had his own and often unusual views on baseball matters. He maintained, against staunch management resistance, that he could pitch nearly every game; it was an incredible concept. But he proved it correct. He doesn't wear sweatshirts, even on cold days, because of studies he has made that suggest it would be counterproductive. That upset traditional baseball thinking. He was one of the first relievers to run in from the bullpen. That was once taboo. And he was under the impression that baseball players are adults. When Harry Walker, his manager at Houston, told him about Astro bedchecks, about what to say to the press, about the Astro dress code, and so on, Marshall finally asked, "And how many times a week may I kill my wife?"

No surprise that Marshall lasted with Houston only a couple of months. In Marshall's rookie year, with Detroit in 1967, he finished with an earned-run average of 1.98 but didn't make the club the next season. He moved on to Seattle, Houston, and Montreal. His reputation always following him. With Montreal, he was named fireman of the year in the National League in 1973. But that winter he was traded to Los Angeles. "There is no doubt," Miller said, "that the powers that be in Montreal did not look kindly on his player association activities."

Marshall says that, although he is proud of the players for their strong stand in the recent strike, he is finished with player association activities.

"I did what I did over the years because I felt it had to be done," he said, "and several times I was even voted team player representative in absentia and I was not unhappy about that. The players once had a total lack of control over their careers, and I thought it was important to take part in changing that.

"But now I want to concentrate strictly on baseball—and forget about the hassles. They've been very distracting to my career. I know I would have been a better pitcher without them."

There is another change with Marshall. He is clean-shaven, no longer sporting his familiar Chester Arthur sideburns and whiskers. "That was only my baseball disguise—I always shaved it off when the baseball season ended," he said, with a smile. "But when the Mets called, they just caught me by surprise."

• • •

Mike Marshall retired after the 1981 season.

THE DIET SECRETS OF RUSTY STAUB

June 30, 1985

Few would argue that the most discerning eater, the most passionate eater, if not one of the most prodigious eaters in all of baseball, is Rusty Staub of the Mets.

"There's a Japanese restaurant with a table for 10 or 11 people," said George Foster, a teammate of Staub's, "but they let Rusty eat at the table by himself."

Staub, an amiable redhead, smiles wanly at the suggested locker-room jibe—a canard, to be sure—that he consumes enormous and indiscriminate quantities of food.

He is, at age 41, a proud professional, both as a restaurateur (he owns Rusty's, the Third Avenue eatery) and as a baseball player. He has played in the big leagues for a remarkable 23 years. He ranks among the career leaders in games played, plate appearances, hits, doubles, and pinch hits, and it was only last season that Foster, it so happens, passed him as the 50th-leading home run hitter in baseball history. (Staub now has 292 homers, his most recent coming last Saturday night when his blast with two on in the seventh inning gave the Mets a 3–2 lead over the Expos.) "Look at the record," Staub says. "Ergo, I must be doing something right."

It is true, and yet to the casual observer it seems obvious that the joys of cuisine—haute or otherwise—play not an insignificant role in his life.

Staub is a large man, standing 6'2½" and weighing 240 pounds (up 40 pounds from when he broke into baseball at 18). And when he comes to the plate—home plate, that is—in a clutch situation, as he often does as the Mets' valued pinch hitter, an ampleness of the midsection, an overlap at the belt, a gentle eave, so to speak, is apparent.

"I don't deny that my body is not the most beautiful in the world now," he says. "But thank God they don't pay me for how I look."

Staub's propensity for gastronomy is widely known. He is a longtime cook who has demonstrated his abundant skills on several television programs, most recently the Robert Morley show, in which Staub whipped up his interpretation of oysters Rockefeller.

"I was told that Morley paid me the ultimate compliment," Staub says, "when he decided not to go out for lunch and stayed and ate all my oysters."

Staub's current lifestyle is one not necessarily designed for maintaining svelte contours. He almost never plays in the field anymore. He has not played regularly at first base or in the outfield since 1981. When he gets on base, a pinch runner is immediately dispatched from the dugout. In late April, the Mets ran out of reserves in the 11th inning and were forced to insert Staub into the outfield. He made a running, shoe-string catch. He later noted: "I didn't sprint for the ball—I don't sprint anymore—but I was chugging as hard as I could."

With his exercise in the field limited, and his love of food strong, one might wonder if Staub must fight his weight. "Constantly," he says. He tries to eat the lighter foods, such as seafood and chicken and simple cooked vegetables.

"But it's hard," he says. "I'll go into my favorite Italian restaurant, and there's this risotto dish that I just love. It's got gravy and porcini mushrooms, and I say, 'Not this time.' But every time I go there I have to get it."

Staub tries to abstain from eating after games, because he knows that late-night consumption puts on weight. He'll often go to his restaurant after a game and sit with some people.

"And they're eating ribs and it smells so good and after a while I just can't stand it anymore," he says. "I call the waiter over: 'Get me some of those damn ribs.'"

Staub also has waged a vigorous battle with a particular brand of ice cream.

"Oh, god, I loved this ice cream, especially the French vanilla and the chocolate-chocolate chip," he said. "I could wipe out a pint rather quickly. I've recently been going more for low-calorie ice creams, but sometimes I just can't resist and dive into a container of the old chocolate-chocolate chip."

As for libations, Staub's ears perk up in a restaurant when he hears the tinkle of the sommelier nearby. Staub enjoys fine wines, particularly red wines from the vineyards of Bordeaux and Burgundy and white wines from Italy.

"Yes, wine has a lot of calories," he said. "So I try to drink moderately. But on an off-day, with good conversation, I'll consume a bottle, sure."

Currently, Staub is particularly mad about a restaurant on Sunset Strip in Los Angeles, where he has met the chef, a personage named Wolfgang.

"The last time I was there I had a wonderful meal that started with fresh tuna raw, followed by a crabmeat salad and swordfish broiled with spices and butter," said Staub. He smiled in recalling the repast, and a look that might be described as rapture shone in his eyes. "I was really into seafood that night."

He has introduced team members to some of the exotic fare that he enjoys, but not all are anxious to seek such delicacies as abalone and coquilles St. Jacques.

Staub noted that some of the younger players are less than particular about food. "I don't want to mention any names but Dwight Gooden and Roger McDowell and Wally Backman will eat anything and everything and anywhere."

Meanwhile, Staub continues to grapple with the problem of satisfying his palate while trying to keep a rein on his waistline. So he jogs every day for nearly half an hour and he works three times a week with an exercise apparatus, and he attempts doggedly to be prudent about what he eats.

"When they wheel the dessert tray to my table, I turn my head away," he said. "But sometimes I peek, and that's my downfall, especially when I see napoleons. I love napoleons."

Ah, and then this renowned gourmet partakes of that gooey, oozy delicacy with knife and fork?

"No, I eat it with my hands," said Staub. "Wear it, who cares!"

• • •

In 1989, Rusty Staub opened a second restaurant on a main thoroughfare in Manhattan, Rusty Staub's on Fifth, and also continued beyond that as a chef and caterer.

FRANK CASHEN'S YELLOW BOW TIE

September 17, 1984

CHICAGO—FRANK CASHEN SAT IN the Mets' dugout in Wrigley Field the other day wearing a yellow bow tie. The Mets' general manager wore more than that, of course, but the yellow bow tie was distinctive.

The bow tie is a kind of personal statement. Cashen is the only general manager in the major leagues who regularly wears one, and, as he sat in the dugout, he may have been the only person in the ballpark wearing one, other than some of the ushers.

"When I'm invited to a baseball affair," he said, "people are disappointed if I don't wear the bow tie. They associate me with it."

The bow tie points out some things about him, and, by extension, about the team he has put together as the guiding light of the Flushing Flashes.

For one thing, a bow tie seems to be, to mix a metaphor, old hat. With this, one is reminded of a line by Saul Bellow, the writer who lives in Chicago only a few miles from Wrigley Field. He once defended old hat by asking, "What's so great about the new hat?"

Cashen has been building a team the old-fashioned way, in fact: from the farm system.

Cashen, now in his fifth season as general manager, could sit and with substantial pleasure watch the team he has put together be in contention for the National League's Eastern Division title into September. They finished in last place last season and were considered likely to remain at that dismal level. In Las Vegas, the Mets were made a 500-1 shot to win the championship.

But they were in and out of first place through parts of this season. They created huge excitement around the city and at Shea Stadium, where the ballpark was vibrating not just from the roar of jet planes overhead, but from the cheers of the crowd as well.

Even though the Mets now have faded and are all but mathematically eliminated from catching the first-place Cubs, the season by almost every measure has been a sweet and unexpected success.

"And most of the players are young and learning," said Cashen. "They've got their best days ahead of them."

There were times early in the year, however, when Cashen might just as happily have not worn a bow tie, and gone incognito.

Not only were the Mets last or next to last in each of the four seasons he had been running the team, but in January he apparently made a mistake and allowed the Shea hero, the terrific Tom Seaver, to be plucked in the free-agent draft by the Chicago White Sox.

Cashen was condemned in some quarters of the news media as being a close but profoundly inferior cousin of the dodo.

He was booed by some fans in attendance when introduced at the New York Baseball Writers dinner in January.

And at the start of the season he and his wife, Jean, were spat upon by atavistic fans when leaving Shea Stadium.

"I could have said that we made Seaver available because of a youth movement or something," he said, "but I was honest and said I had made a mistake."

The apparel oft proclaims the man and Cashen stuck to his style. He wouldn't let fashion dictate his moves—from a personal standpoint on taking heat for a misjudgment, or from his notion of constructing a winning team. He resisted pressure to rush some of the talented young players down on the farm, because he thought it would take time to develop them. The stunning success of Darryl Strawberry last year and of Dwight Gooden and Ron Darling this year have helped prove his point.

The pattern is similar to wearing a bow tie for something like 30 years because this, he found, is what works for him.

"One of the advantages of wearing a bow tie," said Cashen, "is that you never have to worry about dragging it in the spaghetti."

This novel concept did not come to Cashen as in a dream. He arrived at it through hard experience, from trial and error. When he was a newspaperman in Baltimore in the 1950s, he would go into the composing room and lean over the type trays. When he straightened up he would discover that his long tie had become black with ink. One day, he exclaimed to himself, "Eureka, try a bow tie!"

He eventually departed newspapering, took a degree in law from the University of Maryland, and, in an interesting and circuitous career, became an executive with the Baltimore Orioles for 10 years. He took part in the team's championships, helping to build from within the farm system. He attempted the same with the Mets, and had to exert patience.

"Look on the field and you'll see six of our eight starters are from our minor league teams," he said.

The two that aren't are the left fielder George Foster and the first baseman Keith Hernandez.

The first was acquired in a trade after being pursued as a free agent, and the latter was obtained in a deal with the Cardinals. Cashen considers himself flexible in this regard, akin to his bow tie.

"It's reversible," he said. "When it starts to show a little dirt, you just turn it inside-out. They last four or five times longer than regular ties."

He has more bow ties than just the yellow one. He says he has red ones and blue ones and green ones and, well, "about 40 or 50 of them. They're made of a good wool, an excellent fabric, and you can wear almost any color and it doesn't clash with the rest of your clothes."

A visitor asked if the bow tie was real, or clip-on?

With only a slight look of shock (or was it disdain?), he said, "Are you kidding?"

He proceeded to undo the tie and then with the edges hanging from his collar he whipped it back, looping the loops, with no mirror, of course, and fairly skillful fingers.

"There," he said. "Don't know whether that's straight or not."

It was a little off center. Like his team. But tomorrow, like next season, there may be enough time to get it just right.

• • •

Frank Cashen was the general manager and considered the "architect" of the 1986 World Series champion Mets.

MICKEY MANTLE AND KEITH HERNANDEZ, TWO NO. 7s

April 17, 1986

THE CO-AUTHOR, THE ONE who thumps baseballs for a living, autographed books in a corner of the restaurant. He was wearing neither baseball uniform nor sackcloth, but was attired in a black suit and silver tie. His dark hair was brushed as smoothly as his dark mustache.

Keith Hernandez was having a party. Bright streamers hung from the ceiling. Laughter rang out, and there were cool drinks and steamy vittles. This was on an afternoon earlier in the week, at Rusty's, the eatery on Third Avenue, and the occasion for the party was the publication of Hernandez's book, *If At First...*, written with Mike Bryan.

It's a memoir in diary form based on a year that might seem at first glance not to warrant a party. And at a time, with the Mets off to a slow start, that might warrant a more solitary preoccupation. ("We've only played five games, we'll run a streak together soon," said Hernandez.) The book concerns last season with the Mets, viewed by their first baseman: he was going through a bitter divorce; he testified in the Pittsburgh baseball-related drug trials about his, he says, onetime cocaine habit; he stumbled through one of the worst slumps of his career—"there seemed no light at the end of the tunnel." And, though overall he contributed largely to a stirring season for the Mets—he batted .309 with 91 runs batted in, and played a dazzling first base—it was a season that ended in disappointment. The Mets finished three games behind the Cardinals in a tight division race.

But as the title suggests, both the first baseman and the team are, personally and professionally, trying, trying again.

"My book isn't a *Ball Four*," said Hernandez. "That was really a groundbreaking book. It broke the facade of the professional athlete. My book is not a book that will get anybody in trouble." Hernandez said he rarely read books about baseball—his reading often slants toward Civil War subjects—but he recalled one that made an impact. He was a 16-year-old high school junior living in Millbrae, California, in 1970, and enjoyed *Ball Four*, Jim Bouton's rousing recital of life in the big leagues.

Hernandez was struck by some of the sections dealing with Mickey Mantle, whom Hernandez called "my idol."

"It was really different to read about how Mantle came to games hammered," said Hernandez. "I remember one story that told about how he was so hung over from the night before that he couldn't play in the game. But he was called to pinch-hit in the ninth inning and won the game with a homer."

Did Hernandez continue to idolize Mantle after he read the book?

"Yes," said Hernandez, "definitely yes. He was a great ballplayer. What did he do wrong? He drank a lot, and he didn't get enough sleep. But it wasn't like, 'Oh my god, he was shot from the sky.'"

Hernandez said that he had dreams of becoming a big-league ballplayer then, and never believed that because Mantle drank heavily and didn't take care of himself that that was the way to make it to the major leagues. "I didn't look at it as a formula for success," said Hernandez. "Not at all. You marveled that he could do all that nightlife and hit home runs, too. But I guess I understood that he was human, and subject to the same pressures and temptations as anybody else. I also knew that he had to be awfully dedicated, and work very hard to do as well as he did.

"I remember when he came into spring training when I was with the Cardinals. I was about 21 years old then, and I was too awestruck to ask him to take a picture with me. I still wear a number 7 on my uniform because Mantle did." Hernandez has recently been put into a position similar to that of Mantle Revealed. Here was the outstanding baseball player who was something less than perfection.

"Who's perfect? Only one man in history, and He died for our sins," said Hernandez. "Even George Washington was supposed to have his faults."

Even after the revelations concerning Hernandez and the score more of major-leaguers implicated in drug-taking, he doubted that the impact on youngsters would be any greater than when he read about Mickey Mantle's defects.

Should kids admire Keith Hernandez as they had before the dreary headlines?

"What they should see is that I play every day and play hard and play to win," he said. "I think that there's no reason not to admire my performance on the ballfield." The agony and the embarrassment for those involved in the drug-taking has not been lost on other players, said Hernandez. "And maybe good will come out of the bad. I think it already has. I think that because of what has gone on, that ballplayers today are getting smart to it. They know that the pain is not just for you, but for the people around you, especially your family. There are the calls to your mom and dad, preparing them for what's going to be coming out in the papers, and over the television news.

"And when they see that a lot of ballplayers can't get out of the mess without professional help, well, there's a message being sent to America.

"I'm out of touch on the subject, but from what I understand, the days of drugs in baseball have ebbed to nothing. A lot of people in baseball know this. Lee MacPhail, when he was the president of the American League, said this a couple of years ago. But the stuff with Peter Ueberroth is just for publicity.

"When I came in contact with drugs"—a period, he says, that began in 1981 and ended in 1983—"there wasn't all the information around that we have today. We thought it was okay to use for recreation. We believed it was a non-addictive drug, but it proved highly addictive. It was a misconception, a societal misconception. I was stupid, but I wasn't alone."

THIS SWEET SERIES, AND THOSE 16 INNINGS

October 18, 1986

SHE WAS IN A hardware store on Third Avenue Wednesday afternoon when she heard the screams, and with several others, ran outside. Others on the street had stopped, and all were staring up at a man in an apartment window. "The Mets tied the game!" he yelled. "The Mets tied the game!"

Another woman recalled boarding an IRT train at 59th Street, taking a seat, and being unsettled by the look in the eyes of the woman beside her. The woman with the look in her eyes smiled. "The Mets," she said. "The Mets won."

People on the street had gathered around appliance store windows to follow the unfolding of the 16-inning, 7–6 pennant-clinching victory over the Astros, and they huddled around a car to listen to the game on the radio, and they rushed home to turn on the tube.

Moon landings don't get this kind of attention. At least not, it seems, the kind of enthusiasm that was generated by the unexpected developments of this most recent baseball series.

But even though the Mets' victory—an elegant drama, a heart-thumping phantasmagoria—must be savored, there is little time now. It is on to the World Series, and, we wonder, more of the same?

An anchorman on television was asking, "How much more can we take?"

We can take as much as the players can give us in excitement, in thrills, in the grandeur of the game. We are gluttons for great baseball. The question is, how much more can the players take? Now the Mets, and their legion of fans, are to face the Red Sox.

This evening, in the first of the four-of-seven-game series, the question in New York is, can Ron Darling, who majored in Southeast Asian history at Yale and the split-fingered fastball at Shea, still the bats of the mesmerizing Boggs, the grim Rice, the steady Gedman, the plucky Barrett, the venerable Evans, and, when he will make his appearance, the gently ferocious Mr. Baylor, who hits and is hit with alarming clutch frequency?

Or will Bruce Hurst, who follows through with his left leg straight up in the air, which resembles a propeller, meet the challenge of Darling? Will Mr. Hurst blaze his fastball by the likes of the resident Flushing demigods?

"The Mets, they have the finishing touch," said a cab driver in Houston Thursday morning. "And I especially like that Blueberry, no one has to tell him what to do. He's born to it."

His fare didn't correct him and they carried on a conversation about the skills of Darryl Blueberry.

No matter. A berry by any other name would hit and run and throw as sweet.

How much more can the players take? Although their bodies might be sore and aching and sagging, their spirits may be soaring. Sure, they've just completed an energy-depleting series, but they had very few such encounters during the season, as they waltzed to the division title by 21½ games. And so, after these last two come-from-behind extra-inning games that swept them to the title, the glands must surely be charged, the chimes ringing, for the sunny Mookie, the gritty Carter, the dark-eyed, intense, balletic first baseman Hernandez, the resolute Dykstra, the resilient Orosco, the chivalric Knight.

There are some who, having had little interest in baseball, once found it an intrusion; tried, in fact, to uproot a husband from the Game of the Week to shop for a washing machine. Some of them have become passionately involved in the fortunes of the players.

One who was watching television felt the anguish of Schiraldi, who buried his face in a towel on the Red Sox bench after losing Game 4 in relief, and she had hung with tension as Dykstra hit his come-from-behind two-run homer in the bottom of the ninth to win Game 3 for the Mets.

"I root for Schiraldi," she now pronounced, "but I am a Mets fan."

She joins a waxing multitude, but it is not all-inclusive. One dissenter is Dave the Carp, known for many years as a notorious Yankee fan, who was asked if he was depressed about the coming World Series.

"Depressed?" he said. "I'm rooting for my Red Sox."

"Your Red Sox?" shot back his friend. "I thought you hated the Red Sox."

"Well, I do," he said. "But I hate the Mets more. If you grew up in New York, and were a Dodger or Giant or Yankee fan, you could never root for any of the other teams if they got into a World Series. You just hated them too much. Friends of mine say that I'm just being negative. That I should be rooting for the Mets, being a New Yorker. They don't understand." "But you are being negative." "That's beside the point," said Dave the Carp. "Go Red Sox!"

But Dave the Carp admitted that the Mets—and, for that matter, the Red Sox—played playoff games against the Astros and the Angels that were riveting.

"I agree with something Roger Angell was quoted as saying," said Dave the Carp. "He said, basically, 'We've just lived through the greatest week in baseball history.'"

Recently, a story was told about Dan Daniel, the late sportswriter who, as an old man one afternoon several years ago, fell asleep in a baseball press box.

"Shhh," someone said, "don't wake him. He's interviewing Miller Huggins."

One day many years from now, a sportswriter may fall asleep in a press box and someone will say, "Shhh, don't wake him, he's covering the '86 playoffs."

It was a dream playoff. Will this be a dream World Series, too?

RED SOX'S BUCKNER PLAYS WITH PAIN AND ENTHUSIASM

October 20, 1986

BILL BUCKNER OF THE Red Sox runs the bases as if one foot is on a curb and the other on the street. He runs from side to side, lopsided, part hobble, part stumble, part desperation.

He runs with his cap cocked funny on his head, his mustache twitching frantically, his arms pumping laboriously, his curious black high-top spikes digging up the infield.

Watching Buckner run is painful, but not nearly as painful as running is for the 36-year-old Buckner.

His ankles ache, his knees ache, his Achilles' tendon throbs. And sometimes his back becomes an adversary, too.

Before and after every game, he wears ice packs taped to both ankles, both knees, sometimes his back—he pulled a muscle there a few weeks ago—and even his left elbow, which was operated on several years ago to remove a tendon and bone chips.

He looks like a one-man emergency ward.

As for his feet, he saw football players on television last Sunday wearing ankle-high shoes and thought they just might help him, too. So he ordered them.

"It's kind of the last resort," he said. "I can't run any slower so that doesn't matter. I just wanted to feel better. This last month, especially, has been brutal."

A serious question arose over whether Buckner would be physically fit to start in the World Series after having strained his

Achilles' tendon Wednesday night midway through the seventh game of the American League playoff against the Angels. He was removed from the game immediately.

"I couldn't walk on Thursday," he said. "I could jog a little on Friday, and I could run some on Saturday—enough to play."

He went 1-for-4 against Ron Darling, with a single, but he also hit into a double play and struck out.

He was eager to play last night, if he could stand. Several hours before the game, in uniform, he was indeed standing. But he knew he'd have to do more if he was going to be effective against the Mets' starting pitcher in Game 2, Dwight Gooden.

"He's a smart kid," said Buckner. "He has to be, because he doesn't try to strike everyone out anymore. He learned. He knew he'd blow himself out before he was 25 the way he was going. He could have struck out 300 batters this year." Gooden struck out 200. "But he found that he didn't have to. Give him credit. He's still got that great fastball. Don't be fooled."

For Buckner, matters of his health are as prominent in his thoughts as thoughts of hitting against the Mets' mound prodigy.

"The Achilles' is slowly getting better," Buckner said before the game, his high-top spikes clicking on the concrete as he made his way through the underbelly of Shea Stadium to the indoor batting cage. He carried a black bat as though to keep his sore body on balance.

He said that the legs hurt when running the bases, of course, but also affect him at first base. They have hurt him for the last several years.

"I play deeper than I used to," he said. "I have to, because I'm not as quick and don't cover as much ground."

In the batting cage, there are grunts and groans and an assortment of expletives as he transforms into a smooth batting practitioner, the man who for 16 years has hit major league pitching for a career .295 average, the leading batter in the National League in 1980—he was then a Cub—at .324. This season he hit .267 with 18 homers and 102 runs batted in.

"It's been an exciting season, and I really looked forward to this series between our two teams," he said. "It's a dream match-up, and I started getting excited about it when it became a possibility as long ago as June."

After 10 minutes of batting balls thrown underhanded from behind a net some 15 feet away by the Red Sox hitting coach, Walt Hriniak, Buckner, sweating and feeling a rhythm, departed.

He walked back to his clubhouse with a steadfast look in his eyes, and a wobble in his step. Or was it vice versa. He began to open the Mets' clubhouse door when a security guard stopped him. "This isn't yours," the guard said. "Oh," said Buckner, looking at the sign. "I saw the word 'Visitors.' I didn't see the word, 'No.'"

And off he trudged, listing, this time, in the right direction.

Buckner found where he was going, off the field as well as on.

He singled off Gooden in the third to drive in the third run of the inning, and provide the Red Sox with a 3–0 lead. He singled again in the eighth, and wound up 2-for-5 as the Red Sox won, 9–3.

And throughout, the agony for Buckner was apparent. When he made a dive for a bunt in the Mets' half of the third, the ball squirting out of his glove, it gave him even greater pain. He irritated his Achilles' tendon again, but limped through the game until he was removed for a pinch runner after his last hit.

He shambled off the field, as if with pebbles in his shoes, and the players in his dugout met him with handshakes and pats.

In the clubhouse afterward, lumpy with ice packs taped about his body, he was asked how he felt.

"Great," he said, with a tired smile. "We're 2–0."

• • •

Bill Buckner was at first base and, apparently with trouble bending because of injuries, made the infamous error with a ground ball slipping through his legs in Game 6 of the 1986 World Series that eventually led to the Red Sox losing the Series to the Mets.

THERE'S NO STOPPING CARTER

October 23, 1986

BOSTON—AFTER WAITING 12 YEARS to get into a World Series, Gary Carter is not about to allow a couple of sore knees, a single sore thumb, a "beat-up" left palm, a dollop of frustration, a soupcon of fatigue, and assorted other maladies and inconveniences—like the Boston Red Sox—to interfere with his good time.

And tonight he bore considerable responsibility for the Mets tying the World Series at two games apiece, as he whacked two homers in his team's 6–2 triumph at Fenway Park.

"The wall, well, when you look at it," said Carter after the game, "it's intriguing." So intriguing, in fact, that after striking out in the first inning against Al Nipper, Carter hit a ball over the notorious Green Monster in left field in the fourth—driving in the Mets' first two runs—and then struck his second homer over that same intriguing wall in the eighth. He also doubled to lead off the sixth.

He's now had seven hits in 17 times at bat, substantially improved from his trying playoffs, when he was 4-for-27.

This is Gary Carter's 12th full season in the big leagues, and only once, in 1981, had he ever been in a championship series—he was catching for Montreal, which lost in the playoff to the Los Angeles Dodgers.

After the Mets had lost the first two games of the Series to the Red Sox, they came back to win Game 3, 7–1, on the strength of, among other things, two clutch hits by Carter—a double and a single, driving in three runs.

Now, as the Mets went into Game 4, down 2 games to 1, Carter felt the team's chance against the Red Sox starter Nipper were strong.

"Nipper hasn't pitched in any of the playoff games against California," said Carter before tonight's game, "and he had a high ERA this season"—it was 5.38, with a 10–12 won-lost record. He said the Mets weren't "taking Nipper lightly, but the general consensus is that we can beat him."

He said that John McNamara, the Red Sox manager, was starting Nipper because he didn't want to overwork his aces, Roger Clemens and Bruce Hurst.

"If we win," Carter had said, "then it's 2–2, and anyone's series. Just the way it was for us against Houston."

But the Mets could not have had such an upbeat approach for Game 4 if they had not survived Game 3.

"We all knew we had to win that one," said Carter. "We all knew that nobody comes back from 3–0 in a best-of-seven series. So we had to win Tuesday. We knew how important the game was. No one had to tell us. This is a great opportunity, being in the World Series. We may never have the opportunity again in our lifetimes.

"The players talked about it among ourselves. No big thing, but, you know, 'We gotta get this guy, gotta get him early.'" The "guy" was Dennis (Oil Can) Boyd, the Red Sox starting pitcher in Game 3.

There was another motivation. "The Sox were talking sweep," said Carter. "We had won 112 games up to the World Series"—108 in the regular season, four in the playoffs—"and we knew we were better than to be swept."

He said that with a day off called by manager Davey Johnson on Monday, when practice at Fenway Park was canceled, the team was able to rest and ease off from the emotional and physical pressures of the last few weeks, when, in the tough series with the Astros, "every inning, every play, every pitch was crucial." He said he felt the team had suffered a natural letdown.

"There's something else people don't realize about players in the World Series," said Carter. "And that is the added time you have to spend with family and friends, people who come in for these games. You want to make sure they get in all right, that they've got their tickets, and you want to spend time with them."

In Boston for the Series are Carter's wife, Sandy, his father, Jim, his brother, Gordon, and his wife, Linda.

"During the day off," said Carter, "Sandy and I just lounged around all day—never left our hotel room. We watched television, had room service, and napped. It was wonderful."

Not only did he rest his weary mind, but also his weary body: the knees that have undergone surgery in past years, and the thumb that was sprained and caused him to miss a few weeks of the season in August, and the variety of other ailments that forces him to spend a half hour getting taped for a game.

"But it's worth it, to play in the World Series," he said. "It's a thrill. It's a thrill I'll never forget. And I want it to go on and on—and back to Shea Stadium."

It will on Saturday night, for sure.

ALL THE CLASSICAL VERITIES—AND RAZZMATAZZ

October 25, 1986

BOSTON—MAYBE IT WAS FROM lack of sleep, maybe it was something in the scrambled eggs at the hotel's breakfast buffet, or maybe it's simply the occupational hazard: creeping discombobulation. Whatever, a sportswriter working the World Series here discovered himself in an art museum on an afternoon before one of these very late baseball shows that the Series has become.

Before one game, the sportswriter was standing among fans who were watching the horde of his peers on the field.

"Do you have to have a college degree to be a sportswriter?" one fan asked his pal.

"I read their stuff," said the other fan, "and you don't need nothin' to be a sportswriter."

Anyway, now on such strange turf for him as the Museum of Fine Arts, the sportswriter quickly sought a return to familiar ground. He quested for a sporting scene, a Bellows fight night, possibly, or an Eakins sculler.

Neither turned up at the Museum of Fine Arts, and the best he could locate was a kind of combination of both: "Washington Crossing the Delaware," by Thomas Sully.

Then he happened upon another painting, called "Razzmatazz," by Roy Lichtenstein. It's an abstract—which means there's a lot of things going on that are catchy to the eye but not swiftly penetrable to the old cognition.

The sportswriter was reminded that this is the way the World Series has been going as well.

Why had the home team lost each of its first two games?

How could the hobbling Buckner continue to stand, let alone play?

And add a chapter in the mystery of Dwight Gooden.

"Have you second-guessed yourself about starting Gooden with only three days' rest?" a reporter asked Davey Johnson, after Gooden had been knocked out of the box in the Mets' 4–2 loss to the Red Sox in Game 5 Thursday night.

"I'll leave it to the sportswriters and fans to second-guess," he said.

Now, a group of art students and their professor came by and observed the painting. "I think it's handsome," said the professor. "I don't think it's handsome," one student ventured. "I think it's, well, pop. I think it's a parody."

"It may be a parody," said another student. "But I think he cares about composition. I think he's serious."

"Yes," said the professor. "It has all the classical verities—balance, color, humor, pathos...."

So, of course, does the Series, though there are questions of parody here, too: the games are being played so late—for money, Virginia, for prime-time television—that, as John McNamara, the Red Sox manager has said, "I don't know what day it is anymore. Or what night."

As for "World" Series, it's "World" only in that two countries, Canada and the United States, have teams eligible. And for most of the history of the major leagues, it was solely, bombastically an American World Series.

For balance, though, there's still little quite as beautiful at the Museum of Fine Arts or at Fenway Park as Evans working the hit-and-run, or Hernandez executing the 3-6-3 double play, or Hurst pitching out of a jam, going out and in on a hitter—a little chin music in—and up and down.

The color of the Series is made special by, for one thing, the bunting along the infield and upper-deck railings. Roger McDowell, the Mets' relief pitcher, said that "seeing those half-flags will tell me I'm in a special setting." And sometimes fans will rise to the occasion with ingenuity in such "a special setting."

Like the contraption floated from the stands, and eventually landing behind second base and retrieved by the Met shortstop, Rafael Santana. It was, as Dylan Thomas once described something similar, "a silent hullabaloo of balloons."

For humor, there are the circumlocutions and bromides that are inevitable when there is little more to be said about the physical. (Bruce Hurst explained why he didn't show up at the traditional news conference the day before he was scheduled to pitch Game 5: "I'm no prophet. I'm a pitcher. I go out to pitch. I don't know how I'm going to do the next day. So what am I going to talk about?") Meanwhile, there's the stuff about "pitching within myself," which means keeping the concentration, or keeping the faith—same thing?—and "my location," which, after translating the pitcherese, comes out "aim."

In a short series there's the aspect that someone or other's "back" is invariably "against the wall." Unless, as Jim Rice noted after the Red Sox took a 3–2 lead in games, "Our backs are not at the door. Theirs are."

The pathos and drama in the Series revolve often around an unfortunate play—such as Tim Teufel making an error to allow in the only run of Game 1. And the drama builds: can the Mets even the Series, as they return to Shea tonight, and force a seventh and decisive game?

The Series razzmatazz also brings out faces not usually seen at such activities.

"Hey, the secretary of state is supposed to be at the game," someone said.

"We've had a hundred of 'em," said a longtime Washington sportswriter.

In Boston, the Series is the lead Page One news, shoving aside tax legislation, the Soviet Union, and police corruption.

John Kenneth Galbraith, the Harvard economist, said, however, that he has an "exaggeratedly cultural indifference" to the goings-on at the baseball parks.

"I have long ago learned that after three days' close of such events, nobody remembers who won or lost, or cares. There are so many other enjoyments." Like what? "Like taking a really good nap," he said.

Memory was jogged of a moment before the razzmatazz World Series of 1961, between the Reds and the Yankees. Joey, six-year-old son of Freddie Hutchinson, the Cincinnati manager, was interviewed on television.

The interviewer, his voice throbbing with excitement, sweetly said to the lad, "Well, Joey, what do you think about the World Series?"

"It's chicken," he replied.

"But—but your father's in the Series."

"Yeah," said Joey, "he's chicken, too."

DARLING'S BIG DAY DELAYED

October 27, 1986

IT WAS A DARK and leaky afternoon, and Ron Darling turned on the lights and windshield wipers of his 250SL silver-blue Mercedes-Benz, on this, what his wife, Toni, said was "the most important day of his life."

Ron Darling was on his way yesterday to the ballpark. He was on his way to pitch a baseball game, if the weather would behave itself, and the steady rain abate.

Ron Darling was scheduled to pitch the seventh and deciding game of the World Series for the New York Mets, and a city—two cities, certainly, Boston and Gotham—if not much of the nation, would follow this game with profound interest.

"My family's staying with us, and I didn't get to bed until about 3:00 AM," he said. "We got back late from the game, and I was so excited, I still couldn't believe that we had won, that I couldn't have gone right to sleep. But my dad said to me, 'Don't you think you should go to bed?'" Darling said. "It was like I was a kid again, and he thought I should get my rest for the Little League game tomorrow.

"My dad doesn't quite realize that these late games make you go to bed later anyway, and get up later. You can't go to bed at 10:00 PM. It's only the fifth inning."

Darling drove along 34th Street toward the Midtown Tunnel. "My family is nervous, and my wife said, 'I'm fine—just a little hysterical.' She said to me, 'I'm so psyched, I'm not sure I can take it if the game is called.' But maybe because it's raining and we might not play, maybe because of that I feel pretty relaxed. If I was certain of playing then maybe I'd be a wreck, too."

It would be his second start with three days' rest, when normally he rests for four days during the season. He said that even with three days' rest, his arm felt fine. "Sometimes you have to play mind games with your arm," he said. "Even if it's a little tired, or a little sore, you just tell your arm it's okay."

Darling had come through the tunnel and paid the toll. The rain was coming down harder and the fog had grown thicker.

"Right now I don't feel any different than when I'm pitching during the season," he said. "Of course, having faced the Red Sox twice already, I have a pretty good idea of how to pitch to these guys. The time when I get nervous is when I finish throwing in the bullpen and then walk through the corridor under the stands to the dugout. Then I feel my knees get weak.

"And I don't feel right again until I face the first batter. But in that walk, with the spikes echoing on the concrete, you feel very lonely. You wonder if it's going to be one of those days and you're not going to get anybody out.

"For some reason, I was really nervous against Houston in the first game of the playoffs. I didn't really start feeling comfortable until the fourth inning. The worst was probably when I pitched in my first big-league game, in 1983, and the first three batters I faced were Joe Morgan, Pete Rose, and Mike Schmidt. I got them out in order. I don't know how."

Traffic, beyond Darling's moving windshield wipers, was light on the Long Island Expressway. Darling, sitting behind the steering wheel on the right side of the car, British-style, said that maybe he was fooling himself. "Maybe I just don't want to think about the doubts, but you always have them," he said. He mentioned John Tudor, who before pitching the seventh game of last year's Series for the Cardinals said, "If we lose, we'll have nothing to be ashamed of this season."

"John had those doubts, and he expressed them," Darling said. "I was thinking about that yesterday, and when we tied the game at 3–3, Mel told me to leave to avoid the traffic and get my rest for the possible game tomorrow night."

But Mel Stottlemyre, the pitching coach, would understand why Darling didn't leave. "In the 10th, when the Red Sox scored two runs, I felt I had to stay," Darling said. "If we lost, then I'd want to be with the guys. After all we'd gone through, I didn't think we'd be saying, 'Well, it was still a terrific season.' I think we'd be hanging our heads. It would be a great disappointment. After finishing second two years in a row, and coming back in the sixth game of the playoffs, and then the amazing thing that we did in the sixth game of the World Series—after all that, and to lose, would really hurt. You'd just want to run off and get away from everybody."

Passing cars rumbled and hissed on the expressway. Darling, after some thought, said, "Is this the biggest day of my life? I'd say no. I hope it's not. It's the biggest day of my baseball career, yes. My getting married was really a special day. And maybe the biggest day of my life was getting accepted to Yale. I remember I had been accepted to Amherst, and I had set my mind that if I don't get into Yale, well, that's okay. But I got the acceptance and it took me two minutes to decide."

Darling, at age 26, maintains a clear-eyed view of events. He is the son of Ron Darling Sr., a machinist in Worcester, Massachusetts, who for much of his adult life has risen for work at 5:00 AM. "To feed a family of four kids, with modest means," Darling said, "that's pressure, too. I'm not sure if it's any more than pitching in the big leagues—or pitching the seventh game of the World Series. It's just that more people are watching me."

One of those watching him will be Stottlemyre.

"He's a low-key guy and smart," Darling said. "In the bullpen, he'll be watching that I stay calm. You know, you get all jacked up and you want to throw the ball through the wall. He'll start talking about, 'Gee, wasn't that a great game last night...' And pretty soon your mind's off the game and you're into your natural rhythm."

Darling had come off the expressway and pulled into the parking area behind the Mets' bullpen at Shea Stadium. He slipped into a black Hard Rock Cafe jacket. He took an anti-theft contraption from under his seat. He locked it on the steering wheel. "A minute of precaution gives you peace of mind," he said.

Then he dodged the raindrops and hopped over the puddles in the red mud and headed for the clubhouse.

About an hour later, he learned that the game had been postponed.

This afternoon, he would do it all over again.

• • •

In Game 7, Ron Darling started and pitched 3⅔ innings, giving up three runs, all earned, on six hits, with one walk and no strikeouts. The Mets were behind 3–0 when he left the game, but rallied to beat the Red Sox 8–5, and win the World Series.

THE METS AND THE MOON

October 31, 1986

WE KNEW THE BASEBALL game last Monday was important, but we didn't realize just how big it was until Mayor Koch himself was discovered in the Mets' dugout near the end of Game 7, trying desperately to avoid the glare of television cameras.

And if for some reason a camera shot did find him, he wore a Mets hat for disguise.

What was he doing there? Was he offering himself up to Davey Johnson as a pinch hitter? Did he want a baseball? Is he just one of the guys from the neighborhood whom you see pop up in a crowd on television: "Hey, look, there's Weird Lenny—sitting next to the president!"

Or was Mr. Mayor doing what politicians are nurtured from birth to do, that is, glom onto winners?

Regardless, the Mets became baseball champions of North America—of Canada and the United States, at any rate—and politicians and fans exulted.

There are three-pipe problems, 21-gun salutes, and now 500-ton celebrations. Six hundred forty-eight tons of shredded paper, weighed to the last ounce by the Department of Sanitation, were showered on the conquering baseball heroes Tuesday after their 8–5 victory in the seventh game of the World Series, and a city was overjoyed.

The Mets were a delicious entertainment for much of this season, and especially the last few weeks, and many stayed up very late, thanks to the rapacity of the television networks.

"It's such a great game," a man was saying, "and it triumphs despite the businessmen in it."

On the second night after the Mets won the championship, a woman of our acquaintance who only recently embraced the game said she had trouble falling asleep.

"I had to get up early to go to work the next day, but I couldn't stop thinking of the Mets," she said, "and whether Strawberry could have caught that thing." She referred to the ball that dropped out of Darryl Strawberry's glove and over the fence for a home run in Game 7.

"But I finally did drop off to sleep," she said. How did she manage that? "I started thinking about football," she said.

Baseball will be missed this winter, but not the cant of some politicians and fans that has gone with it, especially the talk of "winners" and "losers."

The fact that a baseball team won baseball games is said by some to transform a city, and make it a better place to live. The mayor, when he was finally able to scramble out of the dugout and grab a microphone for dear life, said that the World Series triumph makes us in this city "a family." Perhaps a transitory diversion such as provided by the 1986 version of the New York National League Baseball Club of Flushing, operated by Doubleday Sports Inc., this charming traveling show, might make us love each other as never before, might wish us to turn the other cheek, and clasp our fellow man to our bosom.

And a baseball team that wins a championship might make the city a better place to live, but it seems unlikely (although it has surely made it a harder place to sleep). The essential concerns of city living are unchanged: Is the police blotter still loaded? Was the garbage picked up? Are the streets safe to walk at night? When will the D train show up, anyway?

After the Mets won the 1969 World Series similar thoughts of togetherness were expressed, and more. This was a team that had come into existence only seven years before—they were Casey Stengel's "Metsies"—and had finished 10th, 10th, 10th, 10th, ninth, 10th, and ninth. It was a team that could do virtually nothing right on the field or off. When its star-crossed first baseman, Marvelous Marv Throneberry, turned the knob of the manager's door after a heart-to-heart with Stengel, the knob came off in Marv's hand.

But in 1969 as now, the town went wild as the Mets went from second place in August to overtake the Cubs, beat the Braves in the first regularly scheduled playoff series, and then in the World Series took four games out of five from the powerful Orioles (whose second baseman, coincidentally, was Davey Johnson, the current Mets manager). At one point in 1969, the young, idealistic pitching star of the Mets, Tom Seaver, was supposed to have suggested, "If the Mets can win the World Series, we can resolve Vietnam." Seaver's optimism might not have seemed so misplaced in hindsight; after all, a man had only three months before actually strode on the moon.

Yet the Mets were in a second World Series four years later, and still the United States had soldiers dying in Vietnam. Political passions might have been even greater in 1969 than now. Flower children were strewn through the streets, Kent State was half a year away, and Nixon and Agnew were defiling the two highest elected offices in the United States.

The world was little changed after the Mets won the World Series, other than in those sweet moments of pleasure, and in dreamy memory.

It can hardly be any different for the 1986 Mets.

But they have diverted attention, perhaps even from some of the more important areas—the economy, race relations, even gridlock—and politicians understand and exploit this.

In 1969, as Robert Lipsyte recalled in his splendid book, *SportsWorld*, there was a bitter mayoral campaign and that tense National League pennant race, and a sociologist stood on a midtown New York street corner and questioned 150 passersby, "Who is going to win?"

One hundred and three answered, "The Mets."

The following year, the Mets dropped to third place. Euphoria no more. Fans were disgruntled, and spoke of the Mets' "collapse."

It's doubtful we were any more or less a family after the 1970 season than after the 1969 season, or that we are today.

GRADUATION DAY FOR MOOKIE

May 29, 1996

WHITE PLAINS, NEW YORK—ONE can still picture him in the on-deck circle at Shea Stadium, in a pinstriped Mets uniform, waiting his turn at bat. And when you checked the program, it read, "Mookie Wilson, outfielder."

Today, at the Westchester County Center, he sat in one of the front rows in mortarboard and black gown with yellow cowl, waiting his turn to receive his diploma. And this program, for Mercy College's 58th commencement, read, "William Mookie Wilson, Bachelor of Science degree."

Twenty-two years after he entered college for the first time, as an 18-year-old at Spartanburg Methodist, a junior college in South Carolina, Mookie Wilson, father of three, was able to fill a void he felt within himself, and to fulfill a promise he made to himself and his parents, as well as to his friend and adviser, Julius B. Ness.

Among the more than 600 graduates, Mookie Wilson marched into the huge auditorium and followed a cluster of deans, trustees, and bagpipers.

"Everyone has a void that has to be filled," Wilson said in a reception room before the ceremony. "Getting my college degree was something I felt I had to do. All the home runs and RBIs in the world can't replace that. What I accomplished in baseball was physical. What I accomplished here was intellectual."

Wilson had graduated from high school in Bamberg, South Carolina, and from junior college, but he had been too busy playing baseball to march in either graduation ceremony, too busy working toward what would be a fine 12-year major league career that ended with the Toronto Blue Jays in 1991, when he was 35.

William Mookie Wilson, with his familiar glowing smile looking just a watt or two brighter than usual, was not about to miss today's ceremony. And neither would Rosa, his wife of 17 years, and their two daughters, Ernestine, 11, and Adesina, 10, all in long gold dresses. "We're very proud of him," Rosa said.

A son, Preston, 18, was unable to attend, being otherwise occupied as an outfielder for the Mets' Class A Port St. Lucie (Florida) team.

Does there happen to be a message from Wilson for kids who dream of being professional athletes?

"I think so," he said. "I think they ought to know that there is a life after sports. And that you have to be prepared. An injury at any time could end your career, and after you're finished running and throwing and jumping, you still have a whole life in front of you."

Wilson was a swift 5'10" outfielder for the University of South Carolina when he was drafted by the Mets in 1977. He was 33 credits short of graduating when he entered professional baseball.

"And to think of all the hours I wasted in hotel rooms watching television, when I could have been taking correspondence courses or some other classes," he said. "I might have had a doctor's degree by now."

He was employed in the Mets' community outreach program and as a minor league hitting instructor when, two years ago, he learned about a program for working toward a degree in behavioral sciences at Mercy.

Dr. Ernie Turner, a former pro football player who oversees adult education at the Dobbs Ferry, New York, college, was talking with the Mets about getting some of their athletes into the college program.

Wilson recalled saying, "Hey, I'd like to do that."

Several other local colleges have such programs, and former professional athletes like Dick Barnett, Nate (Tiny) Archibald, Wesley Walker, and Erik McMillan have earned bachelor or advanced degrees from those institutions.

Most of Wilson's classwork was done either by computer or through individual work with professors.

"Sometimes," said Dr. Ann Grow, who taught Wilson in several psychology courses, "he'd call and ask if we could get together at 8:00 in the evening."

Wilson's academic adviser, Shelly Alkin, recalls him phoning from a hotel room in Florida.

"He said, 'I've got some time, could you FedEx that textbook I need?'" Alkin said. "He was wonderful. He was so motivated."

Wilson wound up with mostly Bs in his 12 courses at Mercy. And what did he plan to do with his degree?

"I don't know," he said, smiling. "I've always wanted to have a business of my own. And I've thought that with this background, it might help me in sports as a general manager or some other kind of executive. The world suddenly has more options for me."

As he stood waiting to go on stage for his diploma, Wilson, admitting a slight case of nerves, said to someone nearby, "I might fall down—I'd better be careful."

When his name was announced, there were shouts and whistles for him. He took the diploma in a blue folder and held it aloft, smiling broadly.

The smiles and waves were returned by many in the audience, including one proud woman and two proud girls in gold dresses.

III.

FROM TOM TERRIFIC TO THE 21ST CENTURY

FAREWELL, SWEET PITCHER

June 23, 1987

A WOMAN NAMED PAM working in a restaurant on Second Avenue said recently that she loved Tom Seaver so much in the fifth grade that the kids called her Mrs. Seaver.

A college student named John recalled the day he played hooky from high school to see Seaver in his 1984 return to the Mets, and how watching Seaver come out of the bullpen after pregame warm-ups, and the sellout crowd at Shea screaming their heads off, would always be one of the biggest thrills of his life.

And a writer recalled certain moments in the life of Seaver—that long, low-slung powerful pitching motion, those several comings and goings, that professionalism, that high, boyish giggle—but perhaps what is most quickly recalled is his reaction after the Mets, that "Amazin" eight-year-old team, won the 1969 World Series 4 games to 1 against the Orioles.

Seaver was called "The Franchise," and had won 25 games and lost only seven during the season, had struck out 208 batters and had a 2.21 earned-run average and had won the Cy Young Award, his first of three. "Remember," he said after the Series, "I'm the only Met pitcher in history to have lost a World Series game."

He also won one in that Series, but it was a nice touch, a gentlemanly touch, a touch, in fact, of humility.

Just three weeks ago, Seaver, at age 42 and who apparently was retired but had made no announcement after the Red Sox had let him go at the end of last year, received a phone call during dinner at home in Greenwich, Connecticut. The caller was Frank Cashen, the general manager of the Mets. Would Seaver come out of retirement to help the team, which had just lost two starting pitchers because of injury, and had another coming back from drug rehabilitation? "I'll give it a try," said Seaver. "I don't know," Pam, who loved Seaver, said. "He's a power pitcher, and they get their strength from their legs. And remember, he had a knee operation over the winter." Seaver tried during the last three weeks, pitching in the bullpen at Shea, pitching in an exhibition game for the Mets against Tidewater, pitching in a pair of simulated games with some second-string Mets facing him and other Mets in the field.

"It wasn't there," he said. "I didn't have any good motion on the ball. The batters were hitting it out in front of the plate. And I felt discomfort in my arm, discomfort in my knee."

He had made a decision. He could not meet his high standards. He had had enough.

"No," said Davey Johnson, the Mets' manager, "give yourself more of a chance."

But Bud Harrelson, the Mets' coach, former shortstop and roommate of Seaver, knew that Seaver knew. "He's not going to fool himself," said Harrelson, yesterday at Shea. "And he's his toughest critic. I remember when he'd pitch a three-hitter, and still could be critical of his performance." Yesterday, Tom Seaver announced at a news conference that, after 20 years in the big leagues, he was retiring.

When he walked into the room, with his wife, Nancy, the reporters and cameramen gathered there were quiet. "Hey," he said, rather brightly, "there's no funeral." He looked husky in his blue blazer and youthful with his hair brushed nearly flat against his forehead. Almost like the Tom Seaver one remembered when he first came up to the Mets in the summer of 1967, and recalled to a reporter how frightened he was in his first professional start in Jacksonville, Florida. While warming up in the bullpen, he stopped to stand for the national anthem, and became so nervous that he bent over and got sick. Then he resumed his warm-ups.

"This is a sad-happy time," said Seaver, with a slight reddening of the eyes. "I've got a sense of mixed emotions. In one way this was a fairly easy decision for me to make—after evaluating my performance and the way I've been throwing."

On the other hand, he said, "I would like to have helped this team win the world championship, and I think they have the capabilities to do so."

Oh, what a sweet way to have gone out, one thought. To have Tom Seaver, the living ghost of Tom Seaver, help pitch the Mets to another championship. He would be the cavalry, he would be the Marines, he would be the starting pitcher the Mets so desperately needed.

"I would love to have penciled his name in the lineup," said Davey Johnson. Instead, it ended not triumphantly on the mound, but triumphantly in a football locker room.

He left with pride, he left with dignity, he left with emptier pockets. He had a contract for this season for $750,000, to be paid for the next three months—"just tell us when you're ready to pitch," Frank Cashen told him.

But after three weeks, Seaver in essence tore up the contract. "There weren't any more competitive pitches left," he said. "Got every ounce out of them I could. They were all used up."

Used up in 4,782 innings, 13th on the all-time list. Used up in 647 starts, ninth on the all-time list. Used up in 311 victories, 13th on the all-time list. Used up in 61 shutouts, seventh on the all-time list. Used up with a 2.86 career earned-run average, tied for fourth on the all-time list. Used up with 3,640 strikeouts, third on the all-time list. "I guess it's time now to sit back and reflect on what I've done," he said. "It's been a lovely 20 years. I couldn't have asked for more."

SHORTSTOP FROM THE ZOO

September 24, 1988

THE IMPLICATION WAS THAT either he had rattled the bars and been let out of his cage, or he had escaped.

"Raffy! Raffy! How ya doin'?" shouted Howard Johnson, the infielder, looking up from a card game from across the Mets' clubhouse. "It's a zoo over there, isn't it?"

Rafael Santana, former shortstop for the Mets and current shortstopper for the Yankees, had made a visit on his off day Thursday night to his old teammates, before their game against the Phillies. He wore neither the orange and royal blue of the Mets nor the white and navy blue of the Yankees, but a brown sweater, brown slacks, brown loafers, and a bright smile.

Gary Carter, the curly catcher, saw Santana, planted a kiss on his cheek, and said, "How is it over there in the Bronx Zoo, Raffy?"

To Johnson, Santana said, "We're still in it." Meaning the division race in the American League East.

And to Carter, Santana said, "I'm dealing with it." Meaning Hurricane George, and the winds he blows in the Bronx.

Someone asked him about his elbow. "Messed up," said Santana. "Bone chips?" "Yeah." "How do you throw?"

"With pain. I try not to think about it. Every throw is with pain. But when the season is over I'll take care of it. Either an operation, or rest. The doctors aren't sure." "Does it hurt when you hit?" "No," he said.

"You call that hitting?" said Sid Fernandez, in rubber sweat suit, coming by and throwing a hefty arm around Santana. "If we meet up in the Series, I'll just take care of you with my gas." Fernandez moved toward his locker.

"You call that gas?" said Santana. "I just stick out my bat." He swung out his arms as if batting one of El Sid's fastballs. "And sheeew!" His right hand made a flapping motion, like a baseball winging away.

Funny, though, to see Santana in his old clubhouse, especially on this night, the night in which the Mets would clinch the National League East title.

"Should we vote you a playoff share?" asked Tim Teufel, playing cards with Johnson.

Santana, the regular shortstop on the Mets' 1986 World Series championship team, laughed. "No, I'm not a Met; I'm a Yankee," he reminded Teufel.

On the eve of the Yankees' three-game series with the Red Sox, in which a sweep, or even two victories, would put them within credible reach of the division lead, Santana was saying that the mood of the Yankees was upbeat. "We think we can do it," he said. "We haven't given up. We just need our pitching to come through."

Santana says he is a Yankee now in heart and mind. And followers of the team know that he has been quite a Yankee, playing with such pain, and playing with such consistency, that he even extracted praise from the principal owner of the Bronx Bombers. "I'd love to have Santana on my football team," said Steinbrenner.

But Santana also learned earlier this season—his first with the Yankees—what it is to be wearing the legendary pinstripes in this turbulent day and age.

After contributing to a loss by dropping a routine double-play toss—"It can happen to anyone," he said at the time, "it's just a human error"—he was castigated and thrown into the legendary pinstriped doghouse of the then-manager, Billy Martin.

All Santana did was keep his lip zipped, like the ultimate professional he is, and wait his turn again.

He came back. Now he makes all the proper plays without frills and flourish, is a contact hitter—the kind favored by the current manager, Lou Piniella—and one who is invariably in the middle of rallies, and helps them along.

He is hitting around .240, about what the Yankees had bargained for, and provides the kind of quiet leadership that the Yankees have also come to enjoy from Santana's companionable second baseman, Willie Randolph.

The Yankees had dealt for Santana because they needed some stability at shortstop; Santana is the 30th shortstop the Yankees have had, even more, incredibly enough, than the number of managers or pitching coaches, during the 15-year howling reign of Hurricane George.

The Mets traded Santana for three minor leaguers with potential. They also thought they had their now-and-future shortstop in Kevin Elster.

"You should still be here," someone with the Mets said quietly to Santana.

"It goes that way," said Santana with a shrug.

Santana felt a gentle punch in the back. He turned. "Midgy!" exclaimed Santana. It was Wally Backman, who happens to be the shortest player on the Mets.

"You still playin' baseball?" said Backman. "I'm only 30," said Santana. "Thirty!" said Randy Myers, coming over. "Mel says you played with him!" Mel Stottlemyre is the Met pitching coach, and himself a former Yankee, during the 1960s and 1970s.

"I've got a birth certificate to prove it," said Santana.

"That I'd love to see," said Bud Harrelson, the infield coach.

Someone asked Santana if he missed this clubhouse. "I played here for four years and made a lot of friends," he said. "But," he looked around with a clear-eyed real estate agent's eye, "our clubhouse is bigger."

There was no changing what was, and Santana, upon departing, seemed not to be looking back. The next day he would be in the other clubhouse, the one across town, bigger possibly, and zooier certainly, but his, and one, still, with hope.

SIMPLE WISDOM FROM THE ORACLE OF THE METS

October 5, 1988

LOS ANGELES—BASEBALL IS A cerebral game, certainly, one that in order to succeed takes much quarrying of the nooks and crannies of the noodle. And if there is a baseball player quicker to be contemplative, a ballplayer more ready to be ruminative, a player more eager to excavate the labyrinths of the brain than Keith Hernandez of the Mets, he doesn't come to mind.

It is Hernandez who is such a treat to watch at first base. Keen, swift, adventurous, he virtually transformed the position from a passive one in the infield to nearly the fulcrum.

At bat, he is the hitter who stands out in the clutch, rarely looks silly swinging, that most solid of veterans.

So it is that scribes journey to his locker as seekers of wisdom once flocked to the Oracle of Delphi. And in a moment last night before the first game of the National League playoffs here between the Dodgers and the Mets, Hernandez was asked, "What's the most important thing you have to do against Hershiser?"

Hershiser, of course, was the Dodger starting pitcher, one who had forgotten how to give up runs to the opposition, having broken the major league record with 59 scoreless innings in his last 59 innings.

Now, different people have different reactions upon first having a conundrum fall on their ears. Sherlock Holmes would fire up the first pipe of what would probably be a four-pipe problem. Einstein would pull out the fiddle and ply the bow strings. Keith Hernandez smoothes his luxuriant black mustache. The question concerning Hershiser wasn't quite the riddle of the Sphinx, but it was freighted with topical significance.

"What I'll try to do," said Hernandez, patting the little canopy above his lip, "is see the ball and hit it." He smiled.

Anything else? "Yes, I'll try to get hits, especially when men are on base."

THAT was it. Nothing more, nothing less. But he had reduced this deep, pensive game to bare simplicity.

Against Hershiser, he singled once in three times at bat, and grounded out sharply to first against the relief pitcher Jay Howell to make the first out in the Mets' extraordinary three-run ninth. It was the only three runs the Mets scored, but sufficient to undo the Dodgers by 3–2.

And it was Hernandez who was shouting from the bench for the next batter, Darryl Strawberry, to "be aggressive, be aggressive" at the plate. Strawberry, after fouling off several pitches, lined a big double to score Gregg Jefferies with the first run.

So the Mets were finally beginning to see the ball, and to hit it, as Hernandez said they must, and hit it with citizens on the bases.

Gary Carter's single with two strikes and two out drove in the last two runs.

"It was a dork," Hernandez said of Carter's bloop hit, "but it was justice, because they scored their two runs on dorks."

In the most dramatic fashion ended this first game of the first postseason series between these two most obvious of rivals: the Dodgers, who more than 30 years ago forsook Brooklyn for the greener pastures of bean sprouts and tinsel, and the Mets, who just appeared one day about 25 years ago out of what passes for thin air in Flushing, to attempt to replace the Dodgers, and their expatriate partners, the Giants.

Hernandez was born in San Francisco, was five years old when the Giants and Dodgers went west, and so remembers not the great Dodger-Giant rivalries of Robinson and Furillo and Oisk versus Thomson and Leo and Sal the Barber.

"No, I remember when Marichal hit Roseboro over the head with a bat," said Hernandez, "and I remember when Drysdale was going for the scoreless inning record, the one Hershiser broke, and with one inning to go he hit Dietz with the bases loaded but the umpire said Dietz hadn't tried to get out of the way, and so Drysdale threw again and got Dietz out, and got the record, too."

Hernandez also vividly recalled this other rivalry, the one between the Dodgers and the Mets. One in which this regular season, the Mets have been so dominating, winning 10 of 11 games.

Hernandez, who will be 35 later this month, played in only 95 of the team's 162 games because of a pulled hamstring, and batted .276, his lowest average in 10 years.

Coming into last night's game, though, he said he was good enough to go "full bore." Something he hadn't been able to do of late.

Since the Mets had clinched the National League East flag so early, Hernandez has had the luxury of bringing his injury along slowly.

Against Philadelphia, however, in one of the last games of the season, he beat out a ground ball in the infield, and ran hard because, he said, "we needed the run."

In the last game of the season, against the Cardinals, he went 2-for-4, including a home run. "It felt good, though I've been out too long to really feel in a groove," he said.

When it was mentioned that a predominance of prognosticators have divined that the Dodgers have no chance in the series, citing injuries to Valenzuela and Gibson, and the overall anemia of the L.A. bats, Hernandez philosophically stroked the fringe above his lip.

"Each game in the playoffs and World Series is like opening day," he said. "It's all new. The adrenalin is flowing. You're pumped up. You feel little tingles in the stomach, no matter how long you've been doing this. Of course, they're gone after the first pitch. Then you begin to concentrate, you get into the flow of the game."

And after last night's contest, after the team's stunning come-back win, the oracle of the Mets stroked his mustache and pronounced, "I feel great."

Sometimes even the best of seers utters the absolutely obvious.

WHEN FAT IS BEAUTIFUL

August 7, 1989

FAT WAS GETTING A bad rap. This came from no less an authority on the subject than Mickey Lolich, who was once one of baseball's plumpest pitchers, and one of its best.

From his business establishment, Mickey Lolich's Donut Shop, appropriately enough, in Lake Orion, Michigan, the onetime Tiger, Met, and Padre hurler said, "Throughout my 16 years in the major leagues, whenever things weren't going right, people always looked for reasons. For some, it was 'Maybe they're staying out too late at night,' 'Maybe too many outside interests,' 'Maybe their head's not screwed on right.' For me, it was 'He's too fat.'

"But when I was pitching good, they'd say, 'He's strong as a bull.'"

A call had been placed to Lolich to learn his thoughts concerning Kevin McReynolds. The normally mild-mannered left fielder of the Mets grew quite frosted last week when it was suggested in the media that he had put on a few pounds.

"I've heard reports that I'm 15 pounds over last year," McReynolds said. "It irritates me to have kids come and say, 'You stink, you're fat.'"

McReynolds acknowledged that he wasn't enjoying as good a season at bat as he did last year; and it is a fact that he has put on about four pounds from last season. He tips the scale at 224.

But he said that that is of little consequence. "I'm maybe 10 pounds heavier than when I first signed," he said. He turned professional seven years ago. "If I was any lighter, I don't think I'd be able to play over a long period of time."

He was being used as a scapegoat, he said, for the team's disappointing showing this season. "It's like, 'Country boy signs big contract and gets fat,'" he said.

Lolich has been retired since 1979, after having won 217 games, plus three more in the 1968 World Series, when he led Detroit to a victory over the Cardinals. He admits to adding some weight since his playing days, but he won't be specific. He said that in his last season he weighed 220 pounds, though some observers believe his scale was defective.

"A funny thing now is when I go to the old-timers' games," he said. "All the guys who used to look trim and nice now have pot bellies. They're all out of shape. They look at me and say, 'You haven't changed. You could still go out there and pitch.' It's true. I was just ahead of my time."

Lolich contends that it was simply good "home cooking" that made him develop that famous paunch, and not beer. "Never drank much beer," he said. As for the doughnuts, well, he admits to sampling those with chocolate and vanilla, and with nuts, as well as those filled with "raspberry, strawberry, lemon, butter cream, Bavarian cream, chocolate butter cream."

"But I generally prefer just the plain fry cake, the kind you break in half and dunk in your coffee," he said. "And I don't even eat a lot of those." But does he have an Achilles' heel in regard to cuisine? "Ice cream," he said. "Yes, ice cream." He paused, gathered himself, and then left food for baseball. He said that fat often has nothing to do with ballplaying skills. "I've seen a lot of lean bellies and bad arms," he said. "Don't judge a guy by how he looks. Judge him by whether he gets the job done." He mentioned a couple of portly pitchers who had great success, Wilbur Wood and LaMarr Hoyt. "And look at Rick Reuschel now," said Lolich. "It doesn't look like he pushes away from the dinner table too fast."

As for outfielders, there was, for example, Greg Luzinski. "He was a big man, he was just born that way," said Lolich. "People said he was fat. But if he was a football player, they'd say, 'Some build, huh?'"

And there was Hack Wilson, of the Hall of Fame, who was built like a beer keg, Fat Pat Seerey, who once hit four homers in one game, and two pitchers of a vintage older and possibly even rounder than Lolich, Fat Freddie Fitzsimmons, and Hippo Vaughn. "And don't forget Smokey Burgess," said Lolich. "He was built the way a catcher is supposed to. Try coming down from third and knocking him away from the plate!"

One of the amazing things about Lolich was his speed at fielding. Rod Carew once said that he marveled at how "this chubby guy" bounced off the mound after bunts or taps. "I always thought that the fatter he got," said Carew, "the faster he got."

Lolich said it was a case of perpetual motion. "The bigger you get," he said, "the faster you can roll."

He had been able to camouflage his belly somewhat in the old flannel uniforms. "But in 1970 they came out with the double-knits," he said. "It got kinda bad. Those uniforms just sort of clung to you. Honestly, they didn't do much for me."

If he had it to do over again, would he have tried to stay slimmer?

"Not really," he said. "I was pretty successful the way I was."

Any advice, then, for Kevin McReynolds, or others who are accused of corpulence?

"When people got on me," Lolich said, "I always remembered that old guy with the big belly." Who? "Babe Ruth," he said. "He was my idol."

MORON OF THE MONTH

May 14, 1991

LENNY DYKSTRA WAS NOT the first major league ballplayer to wrap his car around a tree at an odd hour for someone who is supposed to be keeping his body fit for play. Thirty-five years ago in spring training, for example, Don Larsen did the same, at 5:00 AM.

"Either he was out very late, or he was out very early," observed his manager, Casey Stengel. This is a legendary story now, like the Babe pointing to the seats in a World Series game, and a pretty funny story, too.

Like Dykstra, Larsen had been drinking heavily, but unlike Dykstra, the former Mets outfielder now with the Phillies, Larsen was fortunate to leave the scene with only incidental bruises and cuts. Dykstra, with a broken right collarbone, a punctured lung, a broken cheekbone, and three broken ribs, will be out of action for about two months, which is not so funny.

For a long time, and in many societies, drinking has been both a terrible problem and a source of amusement. In America, it gets even merrier. On television you can see beer commercials of ballplayers who play only, it seems, to slake their thirst with a brew afterward, and ex-ballplayers who will punch one another in the nose in the continuing transcendental argument over tastes great versus less filling.

Throughout our sports arenas are signs commending drinking. Now, none of this may be harmful in itself. Sure, there's suggestibility here, but at Yankee Stadium, right next to a beer sign, there's one for potato chips, and ice cream, and gasoline, and a bank. Of course, all of this is legal and it's also part of savoring the good life. Despite high-tech persuasion, though, people around here still usually end up making independent decisions, such as drinking in moderation. That has proved more workable than the government making the drinking judgment for us, as it did during Prohibition.

As for social responsibilities, the beer commercials do say, in lyrical or lite fashion, that we should know when to say when. And occasionally a ballpark public address announcer mentions that drinking and driving might be hazardous.

But Ryne Duren, the former big-leaguer and rehabilitated alcoholic, sometime back had another thought. He said he didn't want to pick on ex-ballplayers—at the time, he was referring to Billy Martin—who made beer spots, and didn't resent the money they made from them. But, he added, "It just bothers me to see ex-athletes making these alcohol commercials because professional sports isn't doing much, educationally speaking, to offset them."

Dykstra ended up relatively lucky. Luckier than Martin, who died in a car crash after drinking, and he had better luck than that enjoyed by Willie Shoemaker, the jockey, who while drinking and driving, crashed his car over an embankment last month and at age 59 is now a quadriplegic. And Dykstra had better luck than Bruce Kimball, the Olympic swimmer, who killed two innocent bystanders while driving under the influence of alcohol.

Baseball, as well as other sports, is in a quandary. Teams get a lot of money from beer advertisers, but they also pay at least lip service to being a good neighbor, and one with a social conscience. But they absolutely don't do enough in regard to the problem of alcohol abuse.

And since they rely on the good will and the cash of the local citizenry, they have a great responsibility. Teams use the city names for profit, they get tax breaks on ballpark rentals, parking lots, and renovations. Meanwhile, they also portray their ballplayers as role models for youth. With this, they ought to do something serious about de-glorifying drinking.

They should display on the neon scoreboard and on telecasts pictures of Dykstra's car smashed against the tree or Dykstra being carried off on a stretcher to the hospital, instead of only showing Dykstra among the leaders in runs scored and on-base percentage.

There should be right alongside the beer sign and after the beer commercials another tableau depicting the number of people killed or maimed around town or in the nation in DWI accidents for the week, the month, the year. Have the Moron Driver of the Month, with photos and stats.

At Shea Stadium, they show film clips of the Three Stooges on their Diamond Vision. Show also a funeral of some young people who met their maker in a drunken-driving car collision. And the faces of the family in tears.

This would not only be a community service, but also a venture in good business. These signs and pictures of alcohol-related deaths would be a boost to help keep fans alive or in the kind of health that allows them to buy tickets to attend games. This could be as much in the self-interest of ballclubs as the ad money they glean from liquor companies. Funny the way free enterprise works sometimes.

GOODEN PONDERS HIS TROUBLES, THE GAME, AND HIS RETURN

April 25, 1995

ST. PETERSBURG, FLORIDA—IT HAD the dusky, surreal atmosphere of a dream state. In that uncertain period between light and dark, the sun had set beyond the trees, and the lights of the small ballpark had been turned on. From the young ballplayers came noises, more like chirps, that rose in the warm, thick air. Nearby, there was the smell of hot dogs being grilled.

This was last week, springtime in Florida, an unlikely and unquestionably grave time for one of those involved in the game.

From a distance one could see a tall, lean man wearing a baseball cap low on his forehead. He stood in the shadows of a brick dugout, his fingers gripping the link fence in front of him, a concern evident in his face. He called words of encouragement to the pitcher on the mound: "Follow through! Keep working!" And after the pitcher allowed a line single, the man prodded the boy: "It's okay. Shake it off. You all right."

Closer, through the haze of the fresh evening, one could make out the familiar features. It was Dwight (Doc) Gooden, who, over the last 11 years, had been hailed as one of the best pitchers in baseball history—a Rookie of the Year, a Cy Young Award winner, a World Series starter, twice an All-Star Game starting pitcher. Dr. K., a strikeout phenomenon like few others.

This scene now was not, however, Port St. Lucie, where, across the state, the New York Mets were training, but North Seminole Park in Tampa, where Gooden was helping coach a Little League team, the Marlins. It is the team on which his nine-year-old, 4'9" son, Dwight Jr., or, Little Doc, as everyone, including Big Doc, calls him, plays. Gooden's other world seemed very far away.

Gooden's bracing messages to the pitcher, a stocky 12-year-old lad with glasses named Kenny, was advice that in his fashion he, Doc Sr., gives to himself daily, during this, his one-year suspension from Major League Baseball for violation of the drug policy.

While Kenny had been at a crossroads in his ballgame, Gooden was at a crossroads in his life. He wants to return to baseball, but his on-field performance has steadily declined: three straight losing seasons culminating in a 3–4 record in 1994, when he pitched just 41 innings. Off the field, things have turned out even worse.

Gooden's latest suspension was imposed in November, shortly after he had twice tested positive for a banned substance, and this shortly after he had been released from the Betty Ford rehabilitation center, and this after he had tested positive during the 1994 season and was suspended from baseball for 60 days.

Earlier this month, a Florida newspaper reported that Gooden had been stopped in March by a highway patrol car and was ticketed for driving his black Mercedes 117 miles per hour at 4:00 in the morning.

The police said there were two bottles of beer in his car, one opened, and a slight smell of beer on Gooden's breath, although he did pass a sobriety test. There was also a revolver in the glove compartment, the police said, unloaded and licensed.

He told a story that he had just come from a basketball game, but the game had been played two days earlier. He said he had taken only a sip of beer to wash down a sandwich—while it is commonly known that someone in drug rehab must stay far away from even the slightest taste of alcohol. Gooden, especially, must keep away because he had admitted that his pattern has been to use drugs after drinking.

"Do you realize that when you're going that fast, you are not only endangering your life, but others as well?" his new representative, the New York attorney Bill Goodstein, asked him recently.

"Yes," Gooden replied.

"You're 31 years old, not a kid anymore," Goodstein said. "You have to take responsibility for your actions."

"I know," Gooden said. "The whole thing was stupid."

Floyd Youmans, in Bermuda shorts, stopped by the Little League diamond, knowing Gooden would be there. Youmans is a former major league pitcher and a former teammate of Gooden at Hillsborough High School in Tampa.

"How does the drug thing start?" Youmans said, repeating a question. "It starts when you're with friends at a party and someone offers you something that they say will make you feel real good. You think, 'Oh, just once. Can't hurt. These are my friends.' Wrong, man, wrong. Pretty soon, you're linin' up coke and sniffin' and wanting more."

Youmans had drug problems, too, and left baseball in 1989 after a five-year career. Gary Sheffield, Gooden's nephew, longtime friend, and slugging outfielder with the Florida Marlins, is four years younger than his uncle and Youmans, but far wiser about the way he hangs out with friends.

"I know Dwight has said that he has to change friends, get out of the environment he was in," Sheffield said. "But a lot of his friends are my friends. And I never tried drugs, and won't. If they approach me with stuff, I take it personally. I've told 'em: 'Get outta my face; I don't do that.' They know if they aren't gone there's gonna be trouble. I think guys like Dwight and Floyd, they weren't leaders. They were followers. I've told Dwight he's gotta be independent."

For the last 10 years, Gooden has packed up his bags from his home in Tampa, and more recently nearby St. Petersburg, and joined the Mets. When he was suspended for six weeks last season, he lost nearly $1.5 million from his contract. Before the drug violation, he was seeking $6 million a year on a new long-term contract with the Mets. Gooden is now a free agent—if he ever qualifies again to play major league baseball—and a risk.

"I'll be back," said Gooden. "It's not if, it's when."

Sometimes he still does pitch. Four mornings a week, he diligently works out with a personal trainer. It is the former head trainer for the Mets, Larry Mayol, who maintains a rigid discipline for two to three hours for Gooden and one or two others at Eckerd College in St. Petersburg.

After work in the weight room, they repair to an otherwise deserted ballfield where some of the exercises include throwing to Mayol behind the plate and then running off the mound to pick up tossed balls like bunts.

"Look at Doc now," Mayol said. "I think he's in the best shape of his life."

Gooden is at playing weight, about 214 pounds over his lithe, 6'3" frame. And when he winds up in shorts and T-shirt and sneakers, there is still that windup, still smooth and still elegant: the high kick, the glove held high, and, from under the Marlins cap from his son's Little League team, eyes fixed on the target, and then the swift, lovely follow-through, though without the customary Dr. K smoke.

The irony is that, for now, Gooden's great talent has nowhere to go except to field that ersatz bunt.

Gooden attends aftercare sessions in St. Petersburg three times a week, and is tested for substance abuse each time. Despite the speeding incident, he reportedly has been clean since November, the last time he was suspended from baseball.

He has a strong support group, including his immediate family, his parents, two sisters, and Sheffield, all of whom live in five of the seven houses on the same street in a waterfront cul-de-sac in St. Petersburg.

Monica, Gooden's wife—who gave birth last December to a boy, Devin, their third child and Dwight's fourth—also works out in the mornings at the college, though she has a different set of exercises, driving there in her green Mercedes, while Gooden will arrive in his fire-engine-red BMW convertible, or the black Mercedes, or a mini-van.

For a while, Gooden, who has grossed an estimated $35 million in his career, was the sole support of his entire family. He is no longer, with Sheffield helping, and there is some income apparently from the husbands of both sisters.

Gooden's life consists of the routine of workouts, aftercare treatment, and family functions, including the Little League games. He says he takes it all very seriously, including the Little League games.

"You hear about all the bad things, but you should also tell about how much effort Doc puts into helping these kids," said Stan McGlamery, a former president of the North Seminole Little League. "He had just come by to watch his kid play, and the manager of the team asked him to help coach the kids. And now he never misses."

In March, Gooden switched agents, going from Jim Neader, who was with him since he signed his big-league contract out of high school in 1982, to Goodstein, in an effort, it seemed, to change his luck, if not his life.

For now, Goodstein believes it is important for Gooden to be in touch regularly with him or his representative in St. Petersburg, Ray Negron. Negron says he calls Gooden a few times a day, and often checks off with him at night.

"You can't be with someone night and day," Negron said, "but it's important for Doc to know that people are looking out for him."

Of course, he must look out for himself, first. "Funny, but that's something Doc really didn't do," said Betty Jones, Gooden's sister and Sheffield's mother. "Dwight is so caring, and so easy. He always wanted to please somebody else before he pleases himself. He always wanted to be well-liked."

It's remarkable the problems that someone who wished to be well-liked, and was, has gotten himself into in the last several years. There were the drugs, the scuffle with police officers in Tampa that resulted in 1986 in a conviction of battery and resisting arrest, and an accusation in 1992 of rape against Gooden and two fellow Mets players, Vince Coleman and Darryl Boston, which the authorities never pressed for what was described as a lack of evidence.

"I've known Doc for several years," said David Cone, the former Mets pitcher now with Toronto, "and I like him very much and consider him a good friend. But I've never felt that I really knew him."

In his first few years, Gooden was handled very carefully by the Mets, closely monitoring the interviews of this most valuable property. Gooden himself says that sometimes he felt as though he wasn't even a part of the team.

Davey Johnson, however, believes it was proper. "A young guy who is vulnerable could get destroyed in some environments," he said.

It is just such a circumstance that Gooden is now seeking desperately to avoid. He is close to his parents. Some people say that his father, Dan, a retired maintenance worker at a chemical plant who is now confined to a wheelchair because of hip problems, and his mother, Ella Mae, are overwhelmed by their son's difficulties. But there are others who, according to Sheffield and Betty Jones, do sit down and talk directly with him.

"But we don't tell him anything he doesn't already know," said Mrs. Jones. "We don't need his money because all of us can work and get by. What we want is for him to be happy, to fulfill his talent, and do the right thing by his wife and children."

Gooden's outward stoicism cracked each time he was suspended. "There were tears," he said. "I cried because of the embarrassment for my family, and the ballclub, and for myself."

There are a spectrum of hurts and indignities now. Gooden was to give a fund-raising clinic for a local hospital, but after the speeding incident the hospital called and canceled, saying the publicity might have been negative.

Goodstein said he has had long talks with Gooden, even reading him some of the strongly critical articles about him after the speeding incident.

"Do you feel good about yourself?" Goodstein asked.

"Not at all," Gooden said.

"Don't you want people to look up to you again, to respect you?"

"I want that more than anything," Gooden said.

Can he get it back, and return to baseball?

"Yes," said Gooden, after a workout under the morning sun at Eckerd College. Sweat dripped down his face. "And I will."

But he had said that before, has made promises before, why should people believe him now?

"My actions will speak for themselves," he said. "They'll see."

Then Dwight Gooden, the former Cy Young Award winner and still wearing the Little League cap from his son's team, climbed into his red convertible and drove off, heading only he knows where.

FICKLE FANS AT SHEA GIVE PIAZZA A BREAK

August 24, 1998

HOME-FIELD ADVANTAGE MEANS, AMONG other things, having the grounds crew put up a hump along the foul lines if you're a bunting team or smooth it if the visitors are; turning up the heat in the visitors' clubhouse to fatigue them before the game; and, of course, having the fans cheer your guys and boo the villains.

And so at a time when the Mets need all the help they can get as they battle for a spot as a wild-card entry in the playoffs, how does one account for fans at Shea Stadium booing Mike Piazza, their leading slugger, with an enthusiasm perhaps second only to their shouts to attract the attention of the beer vendor?

Are they Yankee fans in camouflage?

Or practicing their ghost act for Halloween?

Or hockey fans on a busman's holiday?

For weeks now, Piazza has been booed by so-called Mets fans. That changed quickly, although rather briefly, Saturday afternoon after he hit a grand slam to help the Mets come from behind in a 9–4 victory over Arizona. As he crossed home plate, he received the kind of reception from the multitude that Powerball winners got from their relatives.

There was, however, an overflow sentiment for Piazza yesterday afternoon, as the Mets lost to the Diamondbacks, 4–3. Scattered boos were consistently drowned out by cheers, even after Piazza came to bat for the last time in the game, in the eighth inning. He had gone 0-for-3, including striking out twice with his bat on his shoulder, and left four runners stranded on base—three in scoring position. This time, he lined a ball back that was deflected by the pitcher, and he was thrown out by the shortstop. Still no significant boos. Perhaps this particular Sunday crowd got religion.

And except for rather restrained rudeness when Piazza failed to throw out any of the four runners who tried to steal, it was a relatively quiet day for his brassy critics among the 36,039 spectators.

Up to now, though, the serial booing of Piazza has been a strange phenomenon, as is the whole psychology of booing a performing athlete. In most cases, the guy is trying hard—if not first to help his team win, then at least to pad his statistics, which may come in handy at season's end when his agent talks turkey—or chopped liver, depending on one's numbers—with management.

Bobby Valentine, the Mets' manager, said before yesterday's game, "I don't understand booing. I've never booed anyone myself. I've walked out of some Broadway shows. And I know they whistle at opera and soccer games when the spectators aren't happy with what they're hearing or seeing, but not this wholesale booing, especially for players on the team you're supposed to be rooting for. Some fans just get some kind of gratification from booing."

Does it hurt the player's performance? "It can't help," he said.

"It's something you have to accept," Piazza said. "You try to block it out. But, yeah, you hear it. If you're a high-profile player, you expect more cheers—and more boos. I heard they booed Joe DiMaggio in Yankee Stadium after he held out at the beginning of a season. He was asking for $40,000."

Piazza came to the Mets in late May, after being traded from Florida, where, the week before—in one of these curious baseball transactions—he had been traded after six years with the Dodgers. He had turned down $85 million for six years with the Dodgers—seeking $105 million for seven years. And when he began having trouble hitting with men in scoring position for the Mets, he left fans with a combination of bad feelings. They apparently decided he was greedy for snubbing a sum of money that they would never see in a lifetime, and he had failed to immediately fulfill their RBI dreams. He was resented, castigated, reviled, and, if he still didn't get the picture, booed hoarsely.

An added factor: his arrival necessitated the moving of the popular Todd Hundley from catcher to left field. Hundley, who returned from the disabled list in mid-July, is batting .168 with two home runs. He is not booed.

Piazza, meanwhile, who will become a free agent after this season and may or may not wish to make another deal with the Mets, is the team leader in home runs, with 23, and runs batted in, with 81—with 14 and 46, respectively, for the Mets. He is second to John Olerud in batting, with a .306 average—.320 since joining the Mets. He generally gets grief.

The vicissitudes of fan reaction reminded Valentine of an occurrence in his own career. Valentine was a rookie third baseman for the Dodgers in 1971 and made three errors in one game.

"I was booed unmercifully," he said, "and when the inning ended after the third error, the fans threw seat cushions at me—I guess it was seat cushion day at the park. I was really down about it. I came into the dugout and there was a tear in my eye. I asked Danny Ozark—he was our third-base coach—'Ozie, do you think Bobby Valentine will ever be cheered here?'

"I was first up in the inning, but I was 0-for-3 and I was being pinch-hit for. Just then, the public address announcer said, 'Now batting for Bobby Valentine'—and there was a big roar from the crowd.

"Ozark turned to me as he was leaving the dugout, and said, 'See, they're cheering for you already.'"

Piazza, ruefully, has experienced something of the same.

BOSS' VIEWS ARE MERELY HOCUS FOCUS

July 12, 2000

George Steinbrenner, who is to baseball what Matthew Brady, Edward Steichen, and Richard Avedon are to photography, is an expert on focus.

This is what the Yankees' principal owner said Monday in regard to the Mets' charge after their weekend series that Roger Clemens purposely hit Mike Piazza in the head with a 92-mile-per-hour fastball, and, to a markedly lesser degree, the protested interference call against Met first baseman Todd Zeile.

"They had to take the focus off the fact that they got their fannies handed to them this time," Steinbrenner said. "I'm not sure it wasn't a very wise public relations move for them to take the focus off the way they were beaten.

"I think Bobby Valentine and his people would love to take the focus off that, and have the people forget about the results."

What Steinbrenner—we can just picture him under a black cloth and behind that old boxy camera—is really doing is seeking to return the focus to where he believes the focus has suddenly become unfocused. That is, on his Bronx Bombers. But his defense of his pitcher, while understandable, is tasteless, if not reprehensible.

It is undeniable, of course, that the Yankees beat the Mets three out of four games last weekend, and four out of six in the Subway Series this year. And forget for a moment that an opposing player could very well have been killed, or severely maimed for life, by a pitcher whose salary Steinbrenner pays, but recall his expertise on focus. Examples are long, and legendary:

"I didn't fire the man": Steinbrenner, at a news conference announcing the departure of his manager Dick Howser in 1980. Then in 1987: "Firing Dick Howser and not re-signing Reggie Jackson were the two biggest mistakes I ever made with the Yankees." And there was his defense of himself with his fists in 1981 when attacked by an elevator in Los Angeles after the Yanks were beaten in the World Series by the Dodgers. And every time the Yanks make a stupid trade: "It was my baseball people." And whenever they make a successful move—well, you get the picture.

Now, Steinbrenner may bridle at these observations, saying that that stuff is old hat, but here we are with a new hat that looks very much like the old fedora.

Steinbrenner may very well be a flyspeck this side of objective in his viewpoint. And it says here that the umpire's call, which awarded Chuck Knoblauch second base after initially being thrown out when he was forced to run around Zeile, was the correct one. Either Zeile, dreamily spectating directly in the base path, was canny and knew better, or he's a dolt and didn't. Either way, the Mets' protest of the game to the league office should be dismissed.

The Clemens pitch, which produced a concussion in Piazza despite his wearing a plastic helmet for protection, is another matter. It's a well-worn axiom, as Steinbrenner adds, that fast-ball pitchers "have to live on the inside." And brushbacks are a century-old part of baseball. But that doesn't make it right. Steinbrenner said, "I know Roger, I know he's a family guy who loves his kids, and there's no way a future Hall of Famer like him is going to try to hurt somebody."

Maybe not. But Clemens is famous for hitting people, and is a virtuoso at "chin music." I remember talking to Seattle players a few years ago who said that Clemens hits every Mariner rookie the first time he sees him—"to send a message." A message that can be perilous.

I will never forget Tony Conigliaro of the Red Sox being hit in the face in 1967 with a fastball thrown by Jack Hamilton, who had a reputation like Clemens'. Conigliaro was a 22-year-old slugger, and on his way to a wonderful career. People at the game recall with horror the sound of Hamilton's fastball cracking into his face, like the smashing of a melon.

Tony C. was out for the remainder of that season, and the entire 1968 season. He returned to the game, but his eyesight was impaired, his head forever different from before. He retired in 1975, suffered a heart attack in 1982, and died in 1990 at age 45.

And Clemens' message to Piazza, on a night when his control was superb: you must pay for going 7-for-12 against me lifetime, with three homers.

Pitching inside is one thing. Head-hunting is another. Baseball should no longer tolerate that murderous tradition. And George Steinbrenner, sometimes, yes, a leader in positive ways in baseball, could have judiciously led here, too. But his focus in this grave case was not only self-serving, it was shamelessly distorted.

THE STRAWBERRY SAGA: CALAMITY TIMES TWO

July 31, 2000

In baseball today, the saddest of possible words may well be: Darryl Strawberry.

While hearts go out to David Cone, who, at 37, is wrestling sorrowfully with his baseball career, of not getting the fastball to hum, the slider to slide, among other woes, it is still primarily a baseball story, distressing for this wonderful competitor and achiever, but not tragic.

Strawberry is a different story.

For 20 years—or ever since Strawberry was chosen by the Mets as the first player in the baseball draft in 1980, an 18-year-old left-handed batter out of Los Angeles brimming with such fabulous talent that it was immediately decided by the baseball cognoscenti that he would be the latter-20th-century Ted Williams—we have followed him on the diamond, and in the news.

We have followed him through thin and thick, through his mighty home runs and his mighty strikeouts, both on and off the field.

We followed him as he made his way through battles with drugs, with alcohol, with the I.R.S., with a paternity suit—and losing many of them. He was in rehab centers, under house arrest, released from the Dodgers and the Giants, suspended on a number of occasions, painfully trying to make it all right again, trying to come back time and time again. He became a born-again Christian with a look in his eyes at times that made him appear nearly hypnotized, and then lapsed. He sought to become a rededicated family man, a total team player, and to perhaps hang out with a better class of people than in previous times.

When in 1995 George Steinbrenner gave "this young man"—Strawberry was then 33—"one last chance," he seemed to respond. "I finally feel free," he said at the time. "I just feel I can be me now, and not try to be someone other people wanted me to be. I don't feel the most important thing is to be a baseball star. The most important thing is for me to be a human being."

When Strawberry developed colon cancer in 1998, then beat it into remission and came back to help the Yankees win the World Series last October, he broke down at the ceremony honoring the team on the steps of City Hall and hugged the manager, Joe Torre, who was himself a cancer survivor and who had shown confidence in Strawberry. Regardless of one's feelings for Strawberry, it was hard not to be touched by this moment, by the apparent genuineness of the emotion, of this kind of triumphal culmination of the man's desperate struggles.

And we followed him to this season when, in spring training with the Yankees, Strawberry, now 38, failed a drug test—and was quickly suspended by the baseball commissioner for a year for violating the baseball drug laws again. A year earlier he had propositioned an undercover detective in Tampa, Florida, and had in his wallet a small amount of cocaine—along with photographs of his wife and young children.

And we followed Strawberry to earlier this month when he was seen attending a sex club in Florida, which, in addition to being questionable judgment on his part, may have also been off-limits behavior because of his parole stemming from the sentencing on the cocaine charge last year. We discovered, too, that he had decided to leave early from the drug rehabilitation center he had been in for the last two months. And then, grievously, it was learned that his colon cancer may have returned.

He said he had been in the club only once, and momentarily, while a photograph of him with an, at best, underdressed young woman was seen nationwide. He said he left the rehab center to try to play baseball again to earn a living for his family, amid rumors that, after earning in the neighborhood of $30 million in baseball, he was broke. Maybe all of it is true, maybe none of it is, because he has not always been honest when caught or confronted.

The sadness with Strawberry is, of course, twofold. One is the diminishment of what might have been one of the great careers in baseball, from one kind of sickness that he might have had control over. The other, to be sure, is the tragedy of the physical cancer that he may well have had no control over.

Bobby Valentine, the manager who was a coach with the Mets in Strawberry's first three years with the team, from 1983 to 1985, watched the 6'6" Strawberry arrive in the major leagues with a talent for the ages and then show signs of squandering that talent. "We've all been in places we shouldn't, and maybe done things we shouldn't," Valentine said yesterday. "But many of us say, 'Whew, that was close! I'm not going to do that again.' But Darryl had a supernatural talent, and it may have made him believe he was invincible. He was bigger than anyone else, he was faster than anyone else, he was stronger than anyone else, and so many people were telling him how great he was. Early on, he was skating on thin ice but thought he was walking on water."

Keith Hernandez, a teammate of Strawberry's for most of Strawberry's career with the Mets, which ended in 1990, was himself addicted to cocaine and, in a trial in 1985, spoke about the grip that this "devil on earth" had on him. "I was able to finally go cold turkey to beat it," Hernandez said yesterday while at Shea Stadium for a Mets reunion. "Some can beat it, some can't. An addiction is a terrible, terrible thing. I remember at one point hating it, but feeling unable to control it. I feel sorry for Straw. Basically, I believe he's a good guy. And I'm sure all of his so-called conversions have been genuine, but then something else is working on you.

"But the thing about his not becoming the next Ted Williams, or not living up to his potential, well, he's not the Lone Ranger. It's happened to others—it happened to me to a degree. And that's hardly the important thing at this point for Strawberry. Now he has to deal with the colon cancer again. Who cares now whether he could have hit 500 home runs in his career, or broken Babe Ruth's records?

"Right now, all one can do—should do—is hope he gets healthy again."

THE REVIVAL OF A RED-TINGED RIVALRY STIRS PASSIONS IN THE MIDWEST

October 12, 2000

ST. LOUIS—ENCOUNTERED BY A New Yorker in the lobby of a local hotel, a Cardinals fan was asked if it was true or just hype that people around here don't like New York, and the Mets. "It's genuine," the man said. "New Yorkers can be very antagonistic. When you meet New Yorkers, you get the impression that they don't think there's anyplace but New York."

"Is there?" the New Yorker asked.

"See what I mean!" the man said.

Then the man, Bob Gibson, of Baseball Hall of Fame fame and who still serves as a special instructor to the Cardinals, smiled—that little wicked smile so familiar when he was intimidating big-league batters.

"What's bothered some people around here recently," he said, "is the remarks by some Mets players that they're glad to be playing the Cardinals instead of the Braves in the championship series. Sure, the Cardinals' pitching staff isn't as strong as the Braves', but remember, we just finished beating the Braves in three straight games in the division series.

"And to top it off, I was talking on the phone with a friend in New York, and he said, 'It would be great for baseball if the Yankees and Mets play in a subway World Series.' It would be great for New York, if it's a Subway Series. But not for baseball. The two best teams playing would be great for baseball."

Before it gets to that next step, the Cardinals and the Mets—as well as the Mariners and the Yankees—must settle their affairs. The particular feeling evinced by St. Louis folks toward Gothamites, particularly in the baseball area, reached a boiling point in the mid- and late-1980s, when, in the days before the wild card, the Mets and the Cardinals battled each other bitterly for the National League East title.

The way it was then is the way it is now, as the Mets opened their series at Busch Stadium last night with a 6–2 victory and took the first step toward becoming the NL's representative in the World Series. In the stands, it seemed as though someone had spilled red dye in the washing machines of the capacity crowd of 52,255. Cardinal red was suffused on virtually every blouse and cap and kerchief in sight. And whether it was the color or the competition, their enthusiasms were palpably incited.

But the Mets quickly threw sand in their soup, scoring two runs in the first inning. They added another in the fifth and three more for good measure in the ninth, on home runs by Todd Zeile and Jay Payton. The ballpark during these outbursts was as quiet as a catacomb. The Cards, meanwhile, were toothless, as well as runless, until they scored two unearned runs with two outs in the ninth. It gave the home fans only these few scraps to cheer about—the boosting at this point seemed almost sympathetic—as the Mets took a 1–0 lead in the series.

But things had a decidedly different feel earlier.

"When I walked into the park yesterday," said Ron Darling, a key pitcher for the Mets in the 1980s and now a television sportscaster, "I got goose bumps. We had so many big games here." He recalled that last series between the teams in 1985, when the up-and-coming Mets played in St. Louis in the final week, trailing the first-place Cardinals by three games. The first game was famously won, 1–0, in the 11th inning, when Darryl Strawberry hit a home run so prodigious it seemed like a special-effects gimmick from *Star Wars*.

Darling started that game and went nine innings, giving up just four hits. The Mets won the next day, too, behind Dwight Gooden, but lost the last game, 4–3. The Cardinals won the division, and then the pennant, and the rivalry was in full swing.

Those Cardinals said they weren't getting respect from New York. The Cardinals' manager at the time, Whitey Herzog, who unaccountably relished the nickname the White Rat, said there was a national bias toward the Mets. "Whatever they do gets headlines," he said. "When we do something, it's in the corner of a paper."

Taking his lead, the Cardinals of the '80s became one of the most bilious ballclubs in memory. Their ace pitcher, John Tudor, for one, gave the impression he simply didn't like people, or was it just sportswriters? "All you need to get a press credential for the World Series," he said, "is to show a driver's license." (Was he actually onto something?)

The next year, 1986, the Mets swept the Cardinals in a four-game series in St. Louis early in the season and went on to win the division, the pennant, and the World Series. Two of their stars were the Wunderkinder Strawberry and Gooden. The world was their special oyster. The sky the limit. Whatever became of those two guys anyway?

"Nobody's talked about us all year," Eric Davis, the Cardinals' right fielder, said yesterday, repeating old, familiar lyrics. "Nobody gave us a chance to be here."

Meanwhile, the fans here were cheering their red Lovebirds on. And dissing the guys from the Big City. "Pond scum," is what a local disc jockey, J.C. Corcoran, generously refers to as the Metsies, a term that originated in 1985 and has been happily revived by the local fandom. Corcoran recalled his first trip to Shea Stadium, "It looked like everyone in the crowd had been paroled that afternoon." A New Yorker, in response, might wonder if the man was off his Rocker.

Jose Oquendo, who played for the Mets and the Cardinals in the 1980s and 1990s, and who is now a Cardinals coach, said, "What rivalry? It's just two good teams playing as hard as they know how, trying get to the next level. There's no rivalry. Never been."

There seemed a bit of a pallor to Oquendo, as though the fellow had been living in a cave for some time.

MIKE HAMPTON'S FLUMMOXING

October 11, 2000

ST. LOUIS—LAST IMPRESSIONS CAN be lasting. And the image of Mike Hampton flummoxed on the mound, his Mets cap pulled tightly around his ears and steam rising from them, is memorable. It may be painful for Mets fans to recall, but it may have pertinence to tonight's opening game against the Cardinals in the National League Championship Series. Hampton, after all, is the starting pitcher, the left-hander the Mets are hoping can put them on the freeway to victory. The scene in question occurred in the third inning of Game 1 of the National League Division Series last Wednesday in Pac Bell Park in San Francisco.

Hampton had thrown what he believed to be Strike 3 to the Giants' most menacing batter, one Barry Bonds. The umpire had a different angle—Hampton thought it was from behind a post—and called it a ball. A strike would have resulted in the third out of the inning. Hampton was clearly distracted, his mouth agape within his goatee.

On the next pitch, Bonds whacked a run-scoring triple to put the Giants ahead, 2–1. Two batters later, Ellis Burks hit the foul pole with a drive that scored three runs. And it was curtains for the Mets, at least for the evening.

But they endeavored to come back to win the series and send themselves off to Missouri, with well-pitched games from the other starting pitchers, Al Leiter, Rick Reed, and Bobby J. Jones.

Hampton has been a superb pitcher in his eight seasons in the major leagues, his best being 1999 when he led the National League in victories, with 22, against just four losses, for Houston. He won 15 this season, one short of the team leader, Leiter.

But even fine, experienced athletes can sustain a moment when they suffer dejection, when their minds begin to wander, when they rant at the gods and an official or two for injustices rendered. Then someone triples and someone else parks one into the outfield night.

Had he revisited that inning in his mind over the last week?

"No," Hampton said yesterday. "I thought I made quality pitches to Bonds on the 2-2 pitch and on the 3-2 pitch. Then, you know, it snowballed from there."

Had he learned anything?

"You just try to put it out of your mind," he said. But it would be surprising if he reacted the same way in a similar situation.

Hampton, after all, has a very good memory. He doesn't keep a written file on batters, as some pitchers do. "I don't know if it's ignorance on my part or not, but I basically know every hitter I face. I remember the at-bats they had, when I faced them earlier in the year, the year previous. I really can remember things like that.

"So I use stuff that is stored up a little more than some guys on our team. I know they like to watch videotapes of hitters, study what pitchers are getting them out. But I go on memory."

Bobby Valentine, the Mets' manager, has a memory as well. He was asked if he had considered changing the pitching rotation to throw Leiter first. Leiter, who pitched well despite getting no decision in Game 2, which the Mets won in extra innings, has been regarded as the best and most experienced postseason pitcher the Mets have. "It was the way we opened the season—Hampton first, then Leiter," Valentine said, "and it was the way we opened the playoffs. And all that went pretty well. So I factored all that in and stayed the course."

Was it a big deal to Hampton, for ego or otherwise? "Not really," he said. "I've never put much stock in that kind of thing. The important thing is that I'll get a chance to pitch and show what I can do. These are big games. These are things that we dream about as kids, to be in situations like this, with a legitimate chance to go to the World Series."

Hampton also didn't think that being a lefty necessarily had a great advantage against a Cardinals lineup loaded with left-handers. In the mind-boggling mind games that baseball people play, the strategy would seem to favor the opponents' left-handed thrower.

"It boils down to if you are 'on' that day, regardless if you are right- or left-handed, you got to like your chances," he said.

Of course, there are quality pitches and quality pitches. And there's the reaction to quality pitches when the significant observer behind the plate considers the pitch less than quality. It then becomes imperative to keep one's concentration intact.

TORRE STANDS AT TOP OF CLASS

October 28, 2000

THE MOST BRILLIANT MANAGER in the history of the New York Yankees—at least in this century—sat behind his desk in his Yankee Stadium office yesterday afternoon, a day after guiding his team to its fourth World Series championship in five years. "This one was the toughest," said Joe Torre, and perhaps the most improbable.

This five-game Series victory over the Mets—the team Torre managed from 1977 to 1981 and never finishing higher than fifth—was, in its cockeyed way, as remarkable as any of the other 25 won by the Bronx Bombers, dating back to their first, in 1923, when the mighty Babe was discovering that a ballpark sometimes seemed no bigger than a birdhouse.

No team had ever gone into postseason play as bedraggled, as woebegone, as akin to a car puttering along with four flat tires, as the 2000 Yankees, losers of 15 of their last 18 games at regular season's end.

But now here sat Torre, his deep-set eyes serene after having not gone to bed until 5:00 AM, as aglow within, one might guess, as the diamond-studded World Series ring on his finger. "This one," he said, holding up the ring, "is from last year's championship. I'll change to the new one just as soon as I get it."

One can hardly fault him for wishing to stay au courant. After all, there is that weighty pinstriped legacy looking over his shoulder, literally.

On the wall behind him was a framed drawing of five of the most prominent Yankee managers of the previous century: Miller Huggins, who led the team to six pennants and three world championships in the 1920s; Joe McCarthy, whose 1931–1946 Yankees won eight pennants and seven World Series; Casey Stengel, manager of 10 pennant winners and seven World Series winners, from 1949 to 1960 (and a record five titles in a row); and Billy Martin, who netted two pennants, one World Series championship, and five separate and wacko terms as manager.

Torre was asked where he saw himself in the history of great Yankee managers. He didn't. He said he could hardly believe his luck. "I was in the game for 30 years before coming here," he said, remarking on his years as a player for 16 years with the Braves, the Cardinals, and the Mets, and as a manager for 14 years with the Braves, the Cardinals, and the Mets.

Torre had never been in a World Series game before joining the Yankees in 1996, and was only in the playoffs once, as manager of the Braves. "It was like there was always one step up to reach the top of the hill, but we—I—kept slippin'," he said. "Now it seemed I had someone holding my arm and helping me to reach the top."

As one of his predecessors, Casey Stengel, had said, "I want to thank all the players for giving me the opportunity of being what I was." Torre has expressed equal, if somewhat less convoluted, appreciation for his troops.

Not only did Torre come to the Yankees with a sub-.500 career managing record, so did Huggins and Stengel. McCarthy had won one pennant in five previous seasons with the Cubs (and none with Boston after he left the Yankees). And none of those managers had to contend with division and league playoffs, making entry into the World Series more grueling than ever.

Did Torre believe he was a better manager now than in previous jobs? "I don't," he said. "For one thing, I have an owner who I can talk with directly, who will spend the money to get the players

I think I need. I don't think I had that before. And your players know that, and often respond accordingly."

The Yankees have often seemed to do that. So where lies the art of the manager?

Look to the losing streak. "He was so patient," Billy Connors, the pitching coach, said yesterday. "It was amazing. He never screamed, he never hollered."

He did crack the occasional joke. "I had to laugh, otherwise I'd cry," Torre said. "We weren't playing well because our pitching was poor. I believed it would come around. I had to show patience."

As for Torre's strategy in winning. "I know I get a lot of credit for that," he said. He recalled the last game against the Mets on Thursday night. "I started Vizcaino at second base ahead of Sojo because he hits Al Leiter better."

Jose Vizcaino was lifted for a pinch hitter late in the game. Luis Sojo went to second for defensive purposes. "And then," Torre said, "Luis comes up in the ninth and gets the big hit off Leiter to win the game. I guess that shows you how smart I am."

As smart or smarter than any manager in the 21st century, and he's making a good case for himself for all the other centuries, too. As Casey also said, you could look it up.

FRIENDS AND FAMILY BID AGEE FAREWELL

January 27, 2001

MOUNT VERNON, NEW YORK—It was a sight that the former pitcher Jim (Mudcat) Grant would never forget. It was the spring of 1962 when the 19-year-old bonus baby walked into the Cleveland Indians' clubhouse. "He wore a red tie, a red belt, red socks, and a white seersucker suit that was two sizes too big for him," Grant said this morning in the Grace Baptist Church in Mount Vernon. "His parents had obviously bought it for him and figured he'd grow into it."

It was shortly before the funeral service for Tommie Agee, who died of a heart attack Monday at age 58.

Grant, who had roomed with Agee, had flown from California to pay his respects. "That moment in the clubhouse was the first time I ever saw Tommie," he said. "I said, 'C'mere, I got to talk to you.' I did for him what Larry Doby had done for me when I joined the Indians, and looked something like that. I got him a different tie, a different belt, and different socks." And, he was asked, the suit? "Got rid of it, too."

Art Shamsky and Ed Kranepool, teammates of Agee's on the 1969 Miracle Mets World Series championship team, laughed with Grant.

People were beginning to fill up the pews of this elegant church with its high stained-glass windows and gold organ pipes on the walls. Almost a thousand people would gather to mourn and pass by the open coffin, where the round-faced Agee lay. Beside him was a flower arrangement in the shape of a baseball with the Mets' logo.

"He got an $80,000 bonus," Kranepool said, "but he said he could always have gotten more." Agee was on the phone at his home in Mobile, Alabama, and was negotiating with the Indians himself. "His dad was next to him. Tommie thought he could get a hundred thousand. When it got up to $80,000, his father said, 'Sign now!'"

Agee, who had played briefly for the Indians before going back to the minor leagues, was traded to the White Sox in 1965. Then, in his first full season in the major leagues, he was named the American League Rookie of the Year.

The 5'11", 195-pound center fielder and leadoff hitter ended his 12-year major league career in 1973, with the Astros and the Cardinals, and finished with a .255 career batting average. His most memorable season, to be sure, was 1969, after the Mets had finished in either last place or next to last from their inception in 1962.

His most memorable game was Game 3 of the 1969 World Series against the Baltimore Orioles, when he led off the Mets' first with a homer, then made two great catches, one in left-center and the other in right-center, to rob the Orioles of five runs.

"I was playing right field that game," Shamsky said. "I used to kid him, 'Tommie, you made an easy play look hard, and you've lived off that for 30 years.' And he'd say, 'Yeah, well why didn't you catch it?' And Shamsky's reply, 'Because you called me off the ball.'"

Shamsky smiled at the memory. Agee most recently had been working as an insurance salesman and living in East Elmhurst, Queens. "But a bunch of us who lived in New York were in constant touch," Shamsky said. "We remained a team."

Agee's family came down the aisle and sat down—his wife, Maxcine, and his three daughters. Agee was one of 10 siblings, eight sisters and a brother. There were cousins and nephews and nieces. Donn Clendenon, Tug McGraw, and Bud Harrelson, former teammates, were there, as were Steve Phillips, the Mets' general manager, and Arthur Richman, a former Mets executive and now a Yankee vice-president.

"He was very special to us, his teammates," said Ed Charles, the former third baseman and a key member of the 1969 team, in his eulogy. "I can't ever remember anyone ever saying a bad word about Tommie Agee. He had that disarming smile. We all loved him."

Agee's 13-year-old daughter, J'Nelle, in a gray suit, stepped to the lectern, to pay tribute to her dad. She began to sob in a white handkerchief. The presiding minister, the Reverend W. Franklin Richardson, put an arm around her. "He was a caring father," she said. She talked of a trip to Disneyland with her father and mother and going on the roller coaster and she screamed out of fear on the roller coaster—"and so did he!"

"Mom wanted to go again," she said. "Daddy said, 'No!'"

"The last time I saw him, last Monday, he drove me to school. I said, 'I love you, Daddy.' He said, 'I love you back.'"

She began to cry again, and could not go on. With the help of the minister, she returned to her seat, and the organist struck up "Amazing Grace."

Tonight Tommie Lee Agee's body was taken back to Mobile. He will be buried there Saturday.

BOBBY VALENTINE'S DILEMMA

August 26, 2002

Bobby Valentine is aptly named. The Mets' oft-beleaguered manager, Valentine wears his heart, if not his brain, too, on his sleeve.

He is no Cupid, yet he appears not only to suffer the slings and arrows of outrageous misfortune, but he also zinged some arrows the other day at certain members of his own bat-and-ball troupe. In the wake, that is, of a numbing 12-game losing streak, which ended Saturday night in an improbable come-from-behind ninth-inning victory over Colorado.

It was psychodrama at its nuttiest: the Mets were about to lose (down by 2–1 with two outs and none on in the ninth inning); they were about to win; they were in the throes of blowing it all again; they pulled it out, 5–2. On the bench, Valentine had chewed nervously on his gum, and he bobbed up and down as if riding in a New York City taxicab.

Shockingly, they beat the Rockies again yesterday, 7–4. Two straight! Could this be the start of something belatedly big?

Some say Valentine is the smartest manager in baseball, and if you don't believe that, just ask him. Critics say he overmanages: too many substitutions, too many double switches, the unnecessary squeeze play. Others say he undermanages, especially when it comes to the clubhouse, a not unexpectedly dismal neighborhood over the last two weeks.

The manager must try to do something to stir his charges in the midst of a conglomeration of consecutive defeats, as well as to keep from routinely preparing for the ballpark with a shower and a shave and the donning of a straitjacket.

Last Friday, Valentine was said to come undone, as a tabloid headline had it. He embarked on a tirade after Loss No. 12, to Colorado, after a postgame speech to his players. He said that news reports of his earlier remarks, interpreted to mean that he wanted to be fired, were disgusting, irresponsible, and also wrong.

And he wanted to clear up his remarks in which he had criticized certain players.

"I've never criticized my players in public, and I'll never do it again," he said. Double speak at its richest. But he also said that there were no so-called disciples left in his clubhouse to carry his message. He added that some players were selfish, and later named Edgardo Alfonzo and Al Leiter, each of whom he thought had been too wrapped up in the last year of his contract.

Valentine's shot was seemingly off the mark. Alfonzo and Leiter remain two of the more accomplished and professional players on the team. But some close to the situation believe that Valentine was legitimately disappointed in their lack of leadership, unlike the clubhouse strength they had demonstrated in years past.

In the Yankees' clubhouse, Robin Ventura, traded last December after two seasons with the Mets, discussed Valentine.

"I'd never known Bobby to put down a player in public—or even in private," Ventura said Saturday at Yankee Stadium. "It's a matter of frustration. This is the second year in a row that the team has struggled."

Last season the Mets failed to make the playoffs, after an appearance in the World Series against the Yankees in 2000. This season they have one of baseball's highest payrolls and one of baseball's poorest records, last in the National League East at 60–69.

"Every good team needs a voice in the clubhouse, someone who knows what the manager wants and can convey it to the other players," Ventura said. "Someone or some others who set a standard, who's a presence, someone to be accountable to. But it's hard if you're not going well yourself. Then the problem is first within you. If you're not doing the job, you can't expect to tell others to do it. And that may be the problem with what Bobby called disciples."

For Mets fans, the Bobby Valentine regime, which began in 1996, has been one in which they regularly experienced losing streaks, "swoons" to the faithful. Then the team endeavored to battle back, sometimes succeeding—their heads and bats back in sync—sometimes not. When Valentine told his players Friday, "This is a big hole, and we're going to fight our way out of this," it had the ring of familiarity.

Who must shoulder the burden of responsibility for this season's collapse by the Mets: the manager, the general manager, the players? Reasonably, it's all of the above.

A predecessor of Valentine's with the Amazin's, one Charles Dillon Stengel, once said, "When you're losing, everyone commences to play stupid." That includes management, in the dugout and in the front office.

Stengel was not only wise, he was also prescient. "The only thing worse than a Mets game," he said, "is a Mets doubleheader." Imagine—that was some 40 years ago.

But the Mets' season cannot be called a disaster, except in hyperbole. We are too terribly close to true disasters for that business. So we watch the Mets wrestle with themselves and ground balls, watch their flummoxed manager rail at himself and his gloriously inept team, then we all go to dinner.

As Casey also said, "Now there's three things you can do in a baseball game: you can win or you can lose or it can rain."

• • •

The Mets finished in fifth place in 2002, and Bobby Valentine was discharged as manager.

FROM THREE ANGLES: THE GREATEST AND SMARTEST PLAY EVER MADE

August 13, 2001

SPORTS FANS, COOLING THEMSELVES these sweltering days in a library or, if not handy, a saloon, invariably get around to telling you about the greatest this or the greatest that they've ever seen.

Well, let me tell you about the greatest play in baseball I ever saw—or thought I saw. Few recall it, though it was probably the greatest play Johnny Oates, a second-string catcher and later a big-league manager, also ever saw—or thought he saw.

Oates was the hapless catcher in the play, which was executed by the wondrous and wily Willie Mays, who, incidentally, is in the news, being frequently lauded by his godson, the basher Barry Bonds.

I was reminded of the play at the Baseball Hall of Fame induction ceremonies in Cooperstown last weekend when I saw Mays. I had wondered what he saw on that play—if he even remembered—it being so subtle, so long ago, and his career so crammed with highlights.

The play was not, to be sure, the famous, stupendous, back-to-the-plate catch in center field off the Vic Wertz drive in the 1954 World Series, or any other of Mays' acclaimed swats or snares.

It took place when Mays was a Met, in a Saturday afternoon game at Shea Stadium in July 1973. The great Say Hey Kid was no longer a kid, and no longer even greeting people with, "Say hey." Mays was then 42, and in the 22nd and last season of his brilliant, Hall of Fame career.

In my mind's eye, sitting in the press box that day, this was the situation:

Close game. I forget the opponent. Late innings. Mays is on second base. The batter—don't remember who—drives a hit to right field. Normally, the runner would score from second fairly easily, but this is no ordinary runner. Mays seems to trudge around third, like, well, an old man, and heads home, cap still on head—remember, in his heyday the cap used to fly off his noggin as if he were in a wind tunnel. The right fielder winds up to fire the ball to the plate, certain to nail Methuselah Mays. But incredibly, Mays picks up steam and there he is racing to the plate like, well, the Say Hey Kid!

He beats the throw and is safe at home. Not only that, but because he drew the throw to the plate, the batter is able to go to second, sitting there now in scoring position.

In an instant, Mays had craftily set the whole thing up in his marvelous baseball brain. He obviously had run slowly at first to draw the throw, knowing all along he could make it home.

For me, there is nothing quite as exciting in sports as watching a player—particularly an aging veteran—use his experience, his intelligence, and his considerable if waning skills to accomplish something remarkable under pressure.

One hesitates to use the word *genius* in such endeavors—especially with such folks as Einstein, Picasso, Freud, and Frost looking from the stands—but in my view certain athletes performing certain feats may indeed possess a kind of genius.

Some three decades later I recalled the play to Mays, describing it as I remembered it. Did he remember it?

"Absolutely," he said, in that familiar high-pitched voice. "It was against the Braves. But there's more to it. See, I was on second base and Felix Millan was a runner on first. Ralph Garr was in right field. But not only did I score, I slid into the catcher—it was Johnny Oates—and I pinned him to the ground so Millan could score, too."

I didn't remember the pinning business, so I later called Oates, at his home in Virginia. "I always tell that story at banquets," Oates said. "It was the smartest play I've ever seen, and an embarrassing one for me."

I told Oates what Willie told me.

"I was under the impression that it was a sacrifice fly," Oates said. "And I don't remember him on top of me. He made a perfect slide and took my legs out from under me. My recollection is that I wound up on top of him. But definitely we were lying on the plate, and somehow Willie wouldn't let me get up. The throw went over my head, and the runner behind him did indeed score—how he found the plate with us lying on it I don't know."

To check further for details, I called the Elias Sports Bureau, located in Manhattan, the record keeper for Major League Baseball. Elias confirmed the play essentially the way Mays remembered it, with him and Millan scoring on a hit by Wayne Garrett. (Those runs gave the Mets a 7–6 lead in the eighth, but they lost the game, 9–8.)

I like Johnny's version of the play, I like Willie's, and I still like mine. Take your pick. Along the lines of memorable baseball tales, I've heard two versions of a story that involved Mickey Rivers and Reggie Jackson when they were Yankee outfielders.

Rivers was known to have less than a great formal education, while the voluble Jackson had gone to college. On the team bus one day Jackson was bragging about his I.Q. "Reggie," Rivers said, "you don't even know how to spell I.Q."

Version Two: when Jackson boasted he had an I.Q. of 160, Rivers said, "Out of what, a thousand?"

I recently asked Rivers which version was true. He smiled. "Both," he replied.

Good enough for me.

TRUE HEROISM OUTSIDE OF THE LINES

March 27, 2002

Tom Paciorek was what is known in our society as a sports hero, a baseball star, a golden boy. He played the outfield and first base for six major league teams over 18 sun-burnished seasons—including a brief period with the Mets in 1985. Tom Paciorek played in a World Series with the Dodgers and had a highly respectable lifetime batting average of .282. He hit home runs and batted in clutch runs and made game-saving catches and was cheered lustily in packed ballparks.

He was 6'4" and handsome and had a picture-book family with a wife and six children. When he retired from baseball in 1987, he went into broadcasting. He has been a success in that, too, and is now a television commentator for Atlanta Braves games.

Thomas Marian Paciorek, at age 55, has had it all—including a deep, terrible, humiliating secret.

His unlocking of this secret made him the kind of hero that a mere baseball player could never approach.

Last Friday, in the *Detroit Free Press*, a newspaper in the town where he was born and raised, a story appeared that revealed Paciorek's secret. He said that from 1962 to 1966, from ages 15 to 19—until he went away to college on a football scholarship—he was molested more than 100 times by a teacher in the Roman Catholic school he attended in a Detroit suburb. The teacher became a priest.

Paciorek said he decided to go public when he read last month that the priest, the Reverend Gerald Shirilla, now 63, had been appointed to a northern Michigan parish in Alpena.

"I knew kids there were in danger," Paciorek said yesterday by telephone from the Braves' spring training camp in Jupiter, Florida. "I thought it was time I acted."

Paciorek said he had lost track of Shirilla and believed he had left the priesthood. The local archdiocese, saying there was credible evidence that he had molested boys, barred Shirilla from active ministry in Detroit in 1993. This week, he was removed from St. Mary Roman Catholic Church in Alpena.

Paciorek and three of his brothers told the *Free Press* that Shirilla had molested them. Paciorek said he and his brothers did not discuss the alleged incidents for at least 20 years. Paciorek says he continues to live with shame for never having warned his brothers.

"You try to deny it ever happened, to bury it in your mind"—Shirilla even officiated at Paciorek's wedding when Paciorek was 22—"but you live with horrible emotions, with the loss of self-esteem, with a loss of trust for others," Paciorek said. "I've been in counseling for the last 15 years. Everybody has to work through this. You feel you're on an island alone, that it's only happened to you.

"You don't speak out as a youngster because you feel no one will believe you. And my parents were such devout Catholics that it would have turned their lives upside down. After all, the priest is supposed to represent Jesus on earth. He's the symbol of God in human form. And these priests who are predators are clever. They ingratiate themselves into a family, so as a kid you feel powerless to come forth with the truth. And the kid—he loses his childhood."

Paciorek is a hero because he faced himself. In so doing, he might well have saved some unsuspecting youngsters from the pain, the self-loathing, the victimization that he and his brothers—and so many more who have come forward in recent days and months and years—have suffered from sexual abuse by so-called trusted elders.

Paciorek is a hero the way Sheldon Kennedy was. Kennedy, in early 1997, then with the Boston Bruins, testified openly and courageously against his junior hockey coach who was found guilty of molesting Kennedy and another youngster. Others had testified against the coach, Graham James, behind screens, to conceal their identities.

Speaking out, and facing oneself, takes more courage than hitting a slider or shooting a puck. For those in the public eye who take such a stand, like Paciorek and Kennedy, they display particular mettle. In their macho professions, they may be subjected to ridicule, ignorantly blamed as victims or shunned by frightened employers.

Paciorek said that the night before his story broke, he couldn't sleep. He thought that the next day could be "one of the most fulfilling days of my life, or it could be one of the worst I've ever had."

The response, Paciorek said, has been "really positive."

"I'm still a devout Catholic," he said. "It's not the religion, but some of the people in it, who prey on children. You want to root them out. All of my kids have gone to Catholic schools. I want my grandchildren to go. But I teach them, if there's a problem, any kind of problem, you can come to me. I'll listen."

DAVID WRIGHT IS LEARNING TO RELAX

August 17, 2004

LOOKING EVERY BIT THE young raccoon, 21-year-old David Wright, his eyes framed in eye black, stood in front of his locker at Shea Stadium on Sunday afternoon after the Mets' game against Arizona.

Wright, a third baseman and a major-leaguer now for 25 days, was removing his jersey as he reflected on his experience in the batter's box. He had faced for the first time the formidable, the sometimes unhittable, the famously sizable Randy Johnson, Arizona's 6'10", fourth-in-career-strikeouts pitcher.

"Well, yes, it was a little intimidating," Wright said about facing Johnson, then added, perhaps with a dollop of understatement, "but you have to stay aggressive."

Wright hit a hard ground ball into the hole at shortstop in his first at-bat, but Alex Cintron made a good play on it and threw him out.

When Wright, a solid 6'0", 200-pound right-handed hitter, tried again the next time up, he struck out—one of 14 strikeouts for Johnson. In his third and final plate appearance against Johnson, he flied out to right in the Mets' 2–0 loss.

Although he went hitless against Johnson, Wright displayed a determination and talent indicating a bright future, Mets manager Art Howe said.

"He's holding his own, definitely," Howe said. "I got to know him some in spring training, saw the makeup the kid has. He's getting more and more confident."

Wright began the season in Class AA in Binghamton and played with a flourish. Then, in mid-June, he was promoted to Class AAA Norfolk, where he did well enough that in little more than a month he was wearing a Mets uniform.

As the Mets headed to Colorado to begin a series with the Rockies on Tuesday night, Wright was planning to discuss his at-bats against Johnson with teammates like Joe McEwing, the all-purpose fill-in, and with the Mets' batting coach, Don Baylor—all with an eye to preparing himself for his next encounter with a major league pitcher.

Wright, a first-round draft choice by the Mets in 2001, started slowly when he arrived in the majors July 21, and at one point, his batting average was .167. But he has begun to get the hang of it, and after 88 at-bats, he has a .261 average with six doubles, four home runs, and 13 runs batted in. Not bad for a player who was in Class A ball at this point a year ago.

"I see guys like Piazza constantly working, taking extra batting practice, checking over their DVDs to see how they did against certain pitchers, practicing his throws behind the plate, and it's instructive for me," Wright said, referring to Mike Piazza, who is now on the disabled list with a bad knee. "I mean, a guy like Piazza, the all-time home-run-hitting catcher, and he's still working hard, still learning."

Wright went 0-for-4 in his first game, against Montreal, but the next night he was 2-for-4. Then Wright, of Norfolk, Virginia, began to struggle. Baylor took him into the batting cage and told him to relax. "I was sweating during the games, my muscles were tense," Wright said.

Baylor told him, "Tight muscles are slow muscles. You're getting yourself out. Be aggressive, but not overly aggressive."

In one of his early games, Wright came to bat with runners on second and third and no outs; he swung at the first pitch and grounded out. The runners were unable to advance. "When I came back to the dugout," Wright said, "Piazza came over to me and put his arm around my shoulder. He said, 'Relax.' He said the pitcher was in trouble, not me, and that I swung at the pitch he wanted me to swing at, a slider low and away. Mike said, 'He had to throw strikes in that situation, and you could have waited to get your pitch. You didn't have to expand your strike zone.'"

His approach improved, but for a little while his batting average did not. Howe called Wright into his office. "'Look,'" Wright recalled Howe saying, "'we're happy with your at-bats. It's a matter of time before the balls will start falling in.'"

Wright said, "That was important to hear. It helped relax me."

Although he is considered a strong defensive player, Wright has also had a couple of rough moments in the field and has committed four errors. "He was nervous," said Matt Galante, the Mets' infield coach. "After he'd catch a ground ball, he'd take too many hops. We wanted him to take just one crow hop and throw. He was running with the ball a little bit."

So the education of a rookie is in full swing, with the Mets counting on him to be their regular third baseman for a long, long time. If their expectations are met, it would be a stunning reversal; the Mets' third-base job has seemingly been one of endless auditions, featuring 129 players in their 42-year history.

"He's very inquisitive; it's refreshing," said McEwing, who has become a kind of big brother to Wright. "David wants to know everything about being a big-leaguer, including things like how to tip. But sometimes I have to remind him of certain other things expected of rookies, like having to bring the water bottles for the team onto the plane when we travel. Sometimes he forgets."

Which is understandable when a major-leaguer of just three-plus weeks also has his mind on constricting his strike zone and remembering that it's just one crow hop to first base.

• • •

On September 25, 2012, David Wright, a six-time All-Star singled in the third inning against the Pirates for his 1,419th base hit, snapping a tie with Ed Kranepool to become the Mets' all-time leader in career hits.

LIVE ARM PUTS PELFREY ON METS' FAST TRACK

May 12, 2006

BINGHAMTON, NEW YORK—DEEP IN the heart of the bushes, in upstate New York, a tall, lean young man in a Mets uniform stood on a pitcher's mound.

The ballpark was cozy, a third full with about 2,000 fans present on a pleasant Tuesday evening. In a box seat behind home plate a man jotted down a description of every pitch the young man threw. Some of them arrived in the catcher's mitt at 94, 95, and 96 miles per hour—inning after inning—and the sound of the impact resounded through the park.

The man making notations was Adam Wogan, director of minor league operations for the New York Mets. The player drawing his interest was Mike Pelfrey of the Class AA Binghamton Mets, who was making only his seventh professional start, and who, though a long way from Shea Stadium in distance and environment, just might turn out to be a factor for the major league team this season.

Pelfrey was the Mets' first-round pick in the 2005 draft, and the ninth selection overall, after pitching three seasons at Wichita State. Normally, the Mets would be expected to take their time with a player like Pelfrey, giving him at least a full season in the minors.

But the 22-year-old Pelfrey is more seasoned than any player just out of high school, and with the Mets' starting staff now battered by injuries, the team's eyes, and its radar gun, are zeroing in on him and wondering, what if?

At 6'7", Pelfrey, a right-hander, is three inches shorter than the Yankees' Randy Johnson. And though his delivery resembles Johnson's elongated untangling of arms and legs, he appears more graceful and with similar power.

So, is there a chance that Pelfrey could be pitching in Shea Stadium this season?

"There is the possibility, yes," Omar Minaya, the Mets' general manager, said. "He's got the physical size and talent, but it remains to be seen if he has the mental makeup at this point, whether he pitches with a plan."

At NYSEG Stadium here, Wogan watched closely from his seat behind the protective screen. "He's throwing strikes to spots," he said, obviously pleased.

In the first three innings against the Connecticut Defenders, Pelfrey was perfect, retiring all nine batters. In the fourth, however, he ran into trouble. The ball bounced over the third baseman's head for a leadoff double. Then there was a swinging strikeout on a breaking ball, a pitch that Wogan said showed poise. Pelfrey then hit a batter, allowed a single to right in which the runner was thrown out at the plate, and got a strikeout on a knee-buckling changeup to end the inning.

"He's throwing well," Wogan said.

In the fifth, Pelfrey loaded the bases but got out of the inning with just one run scoring.

"Feel the breeze," a fan shouted as the inning ended with another Pelfrey strikeout.

In the sixth, Pelfrey struck out another batter, on a 96-mph fastball, and as the victim returned to the dugout, another fan yelled, "Don't think you even saw that one."

Pelfrey pitched seven innings. He struck out 10, walked one, and allowed seven hits and an earned run. He did not get the decision in the Mets' 8–3 victory, but he impressed at least one knowledgeable observer.

"Great effort," Juan Samuel, the Binghamton manager and a former major-leaguer, said. "Very impressive. And I liked the way he didn't get rattled and stayed together out there."

Binghamton outfielder Jorge Padilla said of Pelfrey, "Oh, man, he's pretty nasty."

Could Pelfrey help the Shea Stadium Mets today? "I have no idea," Samuel said. "I have to let other people make that decision."

Pelfrey took a similar position as he stood at his locker after the game. "You hear things, but growing up I've heard stuff," Pelfrey said, referring to the lofty expectations others have had for him.

"But you learn to block it out. I try to keep it out of my mind. I only concern myself right now with Double A."

That concern, he said, includes gaining consistency.

"That's what I learned from some of the Mets' pitchers in spring training," Pelfrey said, citing Pedro Martínez, Tom Glavine, and Billy Wagner. "I have to be more consistent, especially on breaking balls and off-speed pitches."

Pelfrey's rise this season has been swift. It started in March, when, as a member of the Mets' 40-man roster after agreeing to a $5.3 million contract, he allowed one earned run over seven innings in two major league spring training games.

He then began the regular season with St. Lucie, the Mets' top Class A team. He had a 2–1 record with a 1.64 earned-run average in four starts, and was quickly promoted to Binghamton. He started his first game for Binghamton on April 29, against the Erie SeaWolves, and went 5⅔ innings, striking out eight and not allowing a run.

In his second Class AA outing, last week against the Akron Aeros, he had a rocky start, giving up four singles in the first inning and two runs. Over all, in four-plus innings, he gave up five runs on 13 hits, with a walk and three strikeouts.

"He came off a bad outing and we wanted to see how he'd handle it," Minaya said in describing the buildup to Tuesday's game. "In the minors, it's important to see kids fail and then have them ask why, so as not to repeat it.

"Mike obviously asked himself some questions, and came away with impressive results. We're monitoring him closely. You'd have to say he's learning."

• • •

Mike Pelfrey was called up to the Mets two months later, in July, and spent part of 2007 with the Mets and in the minor leagues. In 2008, he became a regular part of the team's starting rotation.

IV.

A CLUTCH OF FORMIDABLE RIVALS

MARK McGWIRE: OVER THE FENCE CAME BEFORE OVER THE COUNTER

August 27, 1998

ST. LOUIS—IN MARK MCGWIRE'S first time at bat in Little League in Claremont, California, in 1974, he hit a home run over the fence. He was 10 years old.

When he was in high school, he hit a ball so far that it cleared a 320-foot fence, flew over a vacant lot, and slammed into the wall of a gymnasium an estimated 500 feet from home plate. When Mark McGwire was at the University of Southern California, he whacked 32 home runs in one season (a Pacific-10 record).

In his first full year in the big leagues, in 1987, he belted 49 homers to share the major league lead with Andre Dawson. He has continued orbiting homers, including 58 last season.

In each locale, McGwire, like every other athlete, sought to make himself stronger, fresher, bigger, better. So the consumption of choice began with lemonade, escalated to oranges and candy bars (Snickers, he said), and on to broccoli and—it's true—spinach.

As he draws closer to Roger Maris' single-season home run record of 61—he hit No. 54 against the Florida Marlins last night and has 30 games left in the season—the Cardinals' McGwire has found something even dearer to his heart, and sinews, than fruits, vegetables, and sucrose. This year he began taking andro-stenedione, an over-the-counter supplement that is supposed to enhance the benefits of daily workouts by strengthening body tissues.

Since it is legal in Major League Baseball and in the National Basketball Association—though banned in the National Football League, and by the NCAA and the International Olympic Committee—McGwire is breaking no rules. While the recent revelation that he is using it has sparked a national debate, doctors still are not sure of side effects.

But, an inquiring public asks, is it McGwire or his pharmacist who is responsible for splintering seats in the bleachers and the upper decks?

McGwire has an obvious, and remarkable, natural athletic talent, especially for hitting a baseball long distances, consistently. And he has continued to work on it, and his body, with, apparently, an uncommon devotion. He maintains a rigorous weightlifting program, and is said to study films of pitchers with the intensity of a used-car dealer reading the fine print in a contract.

He has got bigger—and better—as the years have progressed. He stands 6'5" and weighs 245 pounds, some 25 more than when he broke into the major leagues in 1987. His arms are huge, particularly his forearms, which, Bobby Valentine, the Mets' manager, said, "look like calves."

"But that's only part of the story," Valentine said. "He's learned the strike zone better, his swing is more compact, and he's much more disciplined."

His manager, Tony La Russa, derides speculation that it is something other than ability that is responsible for McGwire's blows.

"You can't teach timing in hitting a baseball, especially when you're talking about hitting a 93-mile-per-hour slider," he said. "And if it was just muscle and strength generating those home runs, then you'd have every weightlifter and offensive lineman come off the street and start hitting balls over the fences."

The art and science of hitting a baseball go beyond that. It is a particular skill that may elude even the greatest of athletes—just as the finest chef may meet his bête noire with a pineapple upside-down cake. Michael Jordan, for one, discovered in his adventures in the minor leagues a few years ago that a curveball dipping on the outside corner got the best of him.

"He couldn't generate good bat speed," Valentine said. "He was all upper body."

Other players in the league acknowledge taking Andro, as the supplement is called, including Jason Giambi of Oakland. Giambi has 20 homers, and Maris may rest easily about his challenge. The knowledge, meanwhile, that one substance can enhance performance while another cannot—or to what degree—still meets with conflict within the sports and medical communities.

Yesterday, Major League Baseball and the players' union jointly asked doctors to study players' use of muscle-enhancing pills.

Reckless or harmless, athletes have always sought an edge. Steak, for example, was once considered the best pregame meal. Now it is disparaged, in favor of pasta. Ty Cobb eschewed both in favor of sharpening his spikes.

The bottom line on Mark David McGwire, however, is that he is legitimately the most astonishing home run hitter the world has known since George Herman Ruth ambled to the plate.

BARRY BONDS TALKS, IN HIS FASHION, OF BASEBALL AND STEROIDS

February 23, 2005

SCOTTSDALE, ARIZONA—LOOKING AS BUFF as he has in recent years, wearing a black short-sleeve shirt revealing impressive forearms and a formidable chest, Barry Bonds, age 40 and still the most feared slugger in baseball, said Tuesday that he had nothing to apologize for.

"What did I do?" he said, responding to a question at a news conference.

Bonds, the center of a steroids scandal that has rocked baseball, went on to say that he does nothing but play the game as well as anyone else—if not better—and give fans their money's worth.

In the news conference at Scottsdale Stadium, the San Francisco Giants' spring training home, Bonds spoke for the first time since the *San Francisco Chronicle* reported in December that he told a federal grand jury he had unknowingly used steroids. He spoke sometimes with humor, sometimes defensively, sometimes testily, in his typical forceful voice.

But Bonds, the Giants' left fielder, would not address his testimony in December 2003 before the grand jury investigating the Bay Area Laboratory Co-Operative.

He insisted that the steroids issue had become an issue with the news media, even though alcohol and tobacco "are killers in America, and we legalize them."

Of steroids, he added, "This is just old stuff, like rerun stories. I mean, it's like watching *Sanford and Son*—rerun after rerun after rerun."

Does he view steroid use as cheating?

"I don't know what cheating is," Bonds said. "Is steroid use going to help you in baseball? I just don't believe it. I don't believe steroids can help you, help hand-eye coordination, technically hit a baseball. I just don't believe it, and that's just my opinion."

Bonds was a leadoff hitter when he broke into the majors in 1986 with the Pittsburgh Pirates. He blossomed into a power hitter and set the single-season record for home runs with 73 in 2001. With 703 home runs, he is closing in on Babe Ruth's career total of 714 and approaching Hank Aaron's record of 755.

Beginning in 2000, Bonds' yearly home run output has exceeded all but one of his previous seasons. He has won the past four National League Most Valuable Player Awards and seven over all. Most players' numbers decline as they age, but Bonds', remarkably, have not.

Someone asked Bonds, "Can you explain over the last four or five years your amazing production, your tremendous growth in muscle strength, getting stronger as you get older? Can you finally put to rest...."

"Can I?" Bonds interrupted. "Hard work, that's about it. Now it's rest."

"Rest" was in reference to his knees. Bonds had arthroscopic surgery on his knees in the off-season, most recently on his right knee February 1, and he may not be ready for the Giants' season opener on April 5. He will not be working with the team in Arizona for much, or all, of spring training.

Asked if he was troubled that people were scrutinizing his achievements, particularly his home runs, he brought up his father, the former major-leaguer Bobby Bonds, who died in August 2003.

Bonds said, "The problem with me, my dad told me before he passed away, was: 'Every great athlete that has gone on for great records, everyone knows their story. People have made hundreds of millions of dollars off their stories with them, and protected them.'"

He added, "I'm the son of an athlete. I was the raised to protect my family, keep my mouth shut, and stay quiet."

Bonds looked questioners in the eye on Tuesday, seeking, it seemed, to appear unmoved by the swirl of accusations and questions regarding the possible taint to what is one of the greatest careers in baseball history.

Has any of it taken an emotional toll on him?

"The part that I lose sleep over is my family and my kids," he said.

He added, "I tell my kids: 'You know what, just don't be famous. Let people say whatever they are going to say.'"

Bonds had little more to say about the assertions by the former major league outfielder Jose Canseco in his new book, *Juiced: Wild Times, Rampant 'Roids, Smash Hits, and How Baseball Got Big.* In the book, Canseco suggests that his steroid use inspired Bonds.

"I don't know Canseco, besides hello and good-bye," Bonds said. "It's sad, but I don't bear any weight to anything he says.

"You know, to me, Canseco, you have to come to a lot more than what you're talking about, and fiction, man. There's a whole bunch of books and stories that are out there. Basically, it's just to make money. That's all it is about, making money."

Bonds said he was looking forward to the major leagues' stricter drug-testing policies, which commissioner Bud Selig and the players' union agreed to institute for this season.

"Right now baseball just needs to go forward," he said. "Let us play the game and we will fix it. I think we are all hurting, including myself."

Some have wondered whether asterisks should be applied to any records tainted by performance-enhancing drug use.

But on Tuesday, Bonds said, "You cannot rehash the past, and we'll crush a lot of things out of the sports world. We can go back into the 1800s and basically asterisk a lot of sports, if that's what you want."

SAMMY SOSA: "I DIDN'T KNOW" IS A FAMILIAR REFRAIN

June 7, 2003

CHICAGO—WHEN SAMMY SOSA SAID he didn't know the bat was corked, the line had a resonance that sounded familiar. It was from a 1940s song, "I Didn't Know the Gun Was Loaded."

I didn't know the gun was loaded,
And I'm so sorry, my friend.
I didn't know the gun was loaded,
And I'll never, never do it again.

The song was about a gun-slinging Miss Effie. It contained a plea of ignorance that was essentially the alibi that Sosa, the Chicago Cubs' slugger and irresistible rags-to-riches story, presented after that ignominious moment Tuesday night at Wrigley Field when he hit a ground ball that shattered his bat and exposed the illegal cork in it.

Cork is to baseball what cooking is to corporate books. Glorious until apprehended. Sosa's is the story that Major League Baseball has swallowed whole, the eight-game suspension he received yesterday notwithstanding.

Sosa, the poor kid from the Dominican Republic who became one of this hemisphere's most beloved sports stars, said he used the bat only for batting practice to give the fans a thrill as they witnessed him sending batted ball after batted ball into the beyond. When he strode to the plate in the moment in question against

Tampa Bay, Sosa said, he was so focused on the game that he had no idea that this lighter bat contained cork.

This is a remarkable thing to consider, focus or no focus. Ballplayers are finicky about their bats. They can generally tell within a hairbreadth the length and heft of the bats they order from the manufacturer. In Sosa's case, he has a few manufacturers. Sosa said he had used the bat four or five times in batting practice. And he never marked it, knowing it was illegal?

Sosa broke his bat in the first inning Tuesday night and was ejected after the plate umpire, Tim McClelland, beheld it. Officials of Major League Baseball who were on hand then decided to check all of the bats at Sosa's locker. When they got there, they found 76 of Sosa's bats stacked in the cubbyhole above his locker cubicle. They confiscated them in order to have them X-rayed.

The results, according to Sandy Alderson, executive vice-president of baseball operations for Major League Baseball, were negative. But the bats were not confiscated for several innings, Alderson said. And there was no security in the clubhouse during that time.

What was Sosa doing, if anything, with the bats in that time? What was the clubhouse man doing? Or anyone else? Remember, in the 1994 case of Albert Belle's tainted bat, a Cleveland Indians teammate climbed through the ceiling tiles at Comiskey Park to the umpires' dressing room and switched the bad bat with a legal one. The switch was discovered, and Belle received a 10-game suspension that was reduced to seven games.

Alderson said that the commissioner of baseball, Bud Selig, while wanting "a thorough investigation" of the Sosa episode, retained "a personal affection" for Sosa. Alderson also said that he believed in the Cubs' record-keeping and in theirs and Sosa's willingness to be forthcoming about his bats. Is this not a case also of letting the inmates run the asylum?

The question that Major League Baseball must answer is this: were there more than 77 bats, including the "batting practice" cudgel? It would be a cynical thing if baseball swept the incident under the rug for, as it is said, "the good of the game." The eight-game suspension—which Sosa, not unexpectedly, is appealing, thus allowing him to play in the highly anticipated interleague

Yankees-Cubs series this weekend at Wrigley Field—doesn't answer this.

The notion here is that Sosa was in a slump after a two-week layoff to recover from an infected toe. He had returned to go 2-for-15 with eight strikeouts and no home runs in the three games before the cork incident, and was uncommonly desperate. Even sports gods, when confronted with the possibility of mortality, may descend to plebeian practices. After all, athletes, even superstars, can be insecure. They know that they don't know when their effectiveness is at an end. It's a scary proposition. They want to return to glory as quickly as possible. And, perhaps, by any means possible.

What does all this mean to Western civilization? For one thing, as Andy MacPhail, the president and chief executive of the Cubs, said yesterday, the culture of baseball has never been the paradigm of ethics. "Even Hall of Fame pitchers have scuffed balls," he said. Bats have been corked for decades. A *Wall Street Journal* article in 2001 revealed that Bobby Thomson's famous homer "heard 'round the world" might have been aided by his knowing what pitch the Dodgers' Ralph Branca would throw. The Giants had a man with binoculars in the center-field scoreboard who was stealing the catcher's signs and relaying them to a coach, who swiftly relayed them to the hitter.

MacPhail said he hoped the game would get more ethical. Andy: not until human beings stop playing the game.

Will Sosa now be tainted, will his records be tainted, will every homer he hits in the future be under suspicion?

A vast majority of the 33,317 fans at Wrigley Field on Wednesday night, the night after the incident, stood to applaud Sosa. No surprise. Fans are willing to forgive if you produce. They are rooting for you to produce. They crave their amusements. And for Americans, regardless of what F. Scott Fitzgerald said, there are indeed second acts in public life. Politicians and sports figures, among others, are often disgraced only to reappear in time and regain status and, sometimes, even affection.

So it will be for Sammy Sosa, as long as he draws fans with his homers and "never, never does it again."

JOHN ROCKER: KINDNESS JUST MIGHT UNRAVEL HIM

June 24, 2000

IT IS TIME FOR New Yorkers to turn the other cheek, to embrace with open arms, to bestow a Big Apple welcome to John Loy Rocker, that renowned deep thinker and man of generous insights.

While city officials fear that an appearance by Mr. Rocker with Atlanta on Thursday, when the Braves open a series at Shea Stadium, could result in mayhem, it is to the benefit of Mets fans to perform acts of kindness and civility to the left-handed relief pitcher.

Now, in many circles, opinion on John Rocker is divided. Some believe him to be a moron. Others think that he is an idiot. It's a free country, and their analyses cannot be dismissed out of hand. After all, anyone who paints an entire city—and entire subway cars, for that matter—with one broad, incriminating brush, as Rocker did, may conceivably not be a candidate for the chair at Harvard for the study of enlightenment.

But whether it's necessary to provide, as Mayor Rudolph W. Giuliani said he would, 450 to 500 police officers at Shea for the series—in contrast to the normal complement of 45—is disturbing in more ways than one. And whether it's in the best interests of all concerned to construct a fence and plywood roof to the visitors' bullpen to protect Rocker from rowdiness, as the Mets are planning, is another point that should be thought through.

The contention here is that if Mets fans truly want the best for their team, they should not greet Rocker by hurling boos and batteries at him for having made his now infamous pronouncement in a December issue of *Sports Illustrated*, which included: "Imagine having to take the 7 train, looking like you're in Beirut next to some kid with purple hair, next to some queer with AIDS, right next to some dude who got out of jail for the fourth time, right next to some 20-year-old mom with four kids. It's depressing."

Whether or not you happen to be, say, some kid with purple hair, those statements by Rocker as well as sundry other xenophobic, homophobic, and hirsute phobic remarks, may certainly be construed as offensive. Yet the record shows that ill treatment is no way to behave toward a man who could help the Mets, a team in profound need of assistance.

Look what happened on Wednesday night, for example. Rocker was brought into the game against the Chicago Cubs in the ninth inning, with the Braves behind by 3–1. He came running full bore from the bullpen, as is his wacky wont. The hometown crowd of 44,698 at Turner Field gave him a rousing ovation. Gentleman John proceeded to walk four batters, hit another, allowed one hit, had no strikeouts, and gave up five runs as the Braves went down to an 8–1 defeat.

Remember, Mets fans, that after Rocker's suspension in the early part of this season for his intemperate remarks, he returned to roaring cheers. He was then so thrilled and excited, apparently, by this acceptance, that he pitched his way to the minors, unable to get the ball over the plate. Only recently, after injuries to their bullpen, did the Braves reluctantly recall Rocker. His earned-run average is a gaudy 5.57.

If you are a Mets batsman, this is a man you would be crazy not to want to face.

The genesis of Rocker's remarks to *Sports Illustrated* came while the Braves were beating the Mets in the National League Championship Series last October. Rocker pitched in all six games, generally in tight situations. He gave up three hits in 6⅔ innings, walked just two, and struck out nine. He had two saves in the Braves' four victories. And an ERA of 0.00. He said that

Mets fans had spat on him, threw batteries at him, and visited him with an assortment of other ungallant deeds. And then he went out and destroyed Flushing's darlings.

It's obvious that the worse you act toward Rocker, the better he pitches. And the nicer you treat him, the lousier he plays. It doesn't take an expert in quantum physics to figure out what Mets fans must do to the good ol' boy Rocker.

He had said recently, maybe adding insult to injury, that when he got to New York he was going to take the No. 7 train to Shea. I'd give him a seat.

At the ballpark, I'd toss him a bouquet of flowers, the way they do opera singers and triple-lutz skaters. Lull him into a sense of bliss. Gentleness softens the soul and, more important, enfeebles the sinews in the soup bone.

I'd probably stop short of a ticker-tape parade when Rocker comes to town. But if he pitches like a bum, I'd reconsider. If he performs like a champ again, then I'd go to Plan B: rotten tomatoes.

MAD DOG IS STILL TOP DOG

September 29, 2000

He is called Mad Dog the way bald guys are called Curly, or penny-pinchers are called Big Spenders. It is the flip side of what is. If he were, in fact, a canine, he might be the ultimate thinking man's pooch, a bloodhound, say, or one of those Labrador retrievers who remarkably leads the cops to the packet where the coke is stashed.

If there has ever been a cooler, craftier, better-controlled pitcher mentally, physically, and even facially than Greg (Mad Dog) Maddux, it had to be Sidd Finch, or at least Christy Mathewson. It's true that the surname Maddux lends an alliterative lilt to the nickname, but it fits perfectly for its opposite implications.

Last night, Maddux went to the mound for Atlanta against the Mets looking for this 20th victory against eight losses this season, seeking to extend his scoreless inning streak that stood at 36⅓ innings—the equivalent of four games and a few tokens—and in conspicuous contention for the Cy Young Award, which would be his fifth, a major league record.

But after three perfect innings, Maddux ran into trouble in the fourth when the Mets scored three times, primarily on two infield hits and a single to right by Todd Pratt. It ended Maddux's scoreless streak at 39⅓ innings.

This was less than Maddux's most fortunate outing. He allowed one solid hit in the game, the single by Pratt, while walking two and striking out seven. But the Mets had a 4–1 lead by the time he left after five innings, and wound up winning by 8–2. "I thought I pitched good," Maddux said. "I wanted to pitch good enough to win, but I pitched good enough to lose."

It wasn't just personal gain Maddux was after, but a victory for his team, too. While the Braves have won the National League East title, they still haven't secured home-field advantage in the playoffs.

Maddux was facing a Mets team that was still in seventh heaven, and perhaps with champagne lingering in its hair, after having beaten the Braves the night before to clinch the wild-card berth.

The bill of Mad Dog's cap always looks a little too long, and so the inexpressive eyes in his small, college-sophomore-like face appear to be viewing things from within a cave. He appears no more imposing on the mound than some groundskeeper, no lanky rancor of Randy Johnson, no lean nefariousness of Pedro Martínez, none of the portly desperado of David Wells. Mad Dog stands 6'0", weighs 185 pounds, and doesn't throw as hard as any of the other top pitchers in the game. His breaking balls aren't eye-popping. His weapons, however, are the equivalent of an artist's palette.

"I've been the pitching coach with the Braves for eight years," said Leo Mazzone, "and I'm still in awe of Mad Dog. When he's going well, as he has recently, he can hit the target about 97 percent of the time. He does it with various speeds on his fastballs, and his breaking balls go in on both right-handed and left-handed hitters, and away from them. Most pitchers can do one or the other. And his changeup is virtually pinpoint perfect."

Mazzone also remembers a time when Maddux threw close to Eddie Murray, who made noises that Maddux was trying to hit him. The Braves' catcher, Charlie O'Brien, said to Murray, "Eddie, relax. Mad Dog's control is so good that if he wanted to hit you, he'd hit you right between the eyes."

Maddux, at age 34 and in his 15th big-league season, had a rocky start, for him, this season. Yet in his eight losses, he has given up a paltry 13 runs. He had a 2.91 earned-run average, just shy of his 2.82 mark coming into the season.

"Everything is on the corners, or two inches off," said Jay Payton, the Mets' center fielder. "He never gives you a cookie, one right down the middle. And every time you think you've outguessed him, you gotta guess again."

A few weeks ago, Bobby Cox, the Braves' manager, went to the mound and suggested to Maddux that he walk the next hitter. Maddux told him, no, he'd get the batter to pop to third.

"Bobby came back to the bench," Mazzone recalled, "and the batter popped to third. Bobby said, 'Well, I'll be.' I asked him what it was. And he said, 'Mad Dog told me exactly what he was going to make the guy do—and he did it!'"

Maddux was asked about this Wednesday. "I don't remember it," he said with a sly smile.

"Don't remember it?" came the response. "You who makes a study of every pitch to every batter in every inning?" "Well, it's pitching," Maddux replied. "Hitters read that stuff—or someone tells 'em about it. I don't want them knowing what I'm thinking."

But last night, even against the mighty Maddux, the Mets had an inkling, and that turned out to be more than enough.

THE VICTORY LAPS OF JOHNNY BENCH

July 15, 1983

EIGHTEEN YEARS AGO LAST month, Johnny Lee Bench gave the valedictory speech at his high school graduation in Binger, Oklahoma, a town of 600. The speech was titled "How the Youth of Today Will Be the Leaders of the Next Generation." It is just the kind of subject on which 17-year-old kids are expert.

Bench, the Cincinnati Reds' veteran player, recalled the speech the other day with slightly arched eyebrows. "I don't remember much about it," said Bench. "Oh, there were some vague thoughts about making the world a better place to live. But I was a naive kid, and I only had thoughts of becoming a major league baseball player." He smiled. "I decided very early to back out on the presidency."

Bench, as the sporting public knows, succeeded mightily in his ambition. He became one of the best catchers in the history of the game.

The Reds are making their last swing of the season through the Eastern cities of the National League, and it is Johnny Bench's last swing as a player. Last night's game against the Mets was his last in New York. He has announced his retirement at the end of the season.

And now, in the 16th and final season of his major league career, he is taking curtain calls, perhaps not with the frequency of Sarah Bernhardt's numerous farewell tours, but receiving, one might imagine, similar warmth and admiration.

Before Wednesday night's game at Shea Stadium, a decorous ceremony was held at home plate, and Tom Seaver, a friend, a onetime teammate, and a once and current opponent, presented him a "token of appreciation" from the Mets, a diamond-studded pendant in the shape of his uniform number, 5. The fans and the players on both teams stood and applauded generously.

And Bench, at age 35, doffed his long-billed red cap and waved, revealing a still-young-looking face and, as he turned, a small bald patch on the back of his head.

After another night in New York, the club would be on to Philadelphia, where some of Bench's teammates with the old Big Red Machine now play: Pete Rose, Tony Perez, Joe Morgan. "I know the Phillies are planning a little something, too," said Bench.

Last week, he was honored along with Carl Yastrzemski, also retiring, at the All-Star Game in Chicago. Many of the old Hall of Famers were there, and at a luncheon they gave Bench a standing ovation. Bill Dickey, the former star catcher of the Yankees, came by and said to Bench, "Joining the rest of us, huh?"

"That," Bench recalled later, "was a real thrill." On September 17, the Reds are playing Houston at Riverfront Stadium in Cincinnati, and it has been designated Johnny Bench Night. Bench is scheduled to be behind the plate, for old times' sake.

Two years ago, after 13 seasons as a catcher, he told the club that he could no longer play there. He would be available for third base and first base. Backstopping had taken a terrible toll on his body: his knees ached, his back ached, his shoulders and throwing elbow ached. "I've been shot up with so many painkillers to stay in the lineup," he said, "that if I were a racehorse I'd be illegal."

He had caught 100 games or more for 13 straight seasons, a major league record he shares with Dickey. For his last game as a catcher, he'll have to warm up his body and especially his arm for two weeks in advance, he said wryly. "Nowadays," he added, thinking of trying to throw out stealers, "all the base runners wear track shoes."

And now his playing career is nearly ended, a career that was begun and nurtured in the tiny town of Binger. "You start out not being able to go to the proms or buzzing around all day in a car, because you've got to be on the field, practicing, practicing," Bench recalled, "and dreaming about becoming Mickey Mantle or Willie Mays."

Indeed, he became a national sports figure, much as they had. But what about the valediction, about becoming a leader of the next generation? Did he think he had fulfilled some of that promise as a baseball player?

"When people heard I was retiring," said Bench, "I got a lot of letters from kids and adults saying, 'Thanks.' They said I had helped them get over some humps, especially after I had had surgery for lung cancer in 1972. I was only 25 years old. And I came back to play regularly. I think that gave some people encouragement, seeing that if I didn't let something like that get me down—well, too down, because I was scared—then they wouldn't let whatever problems they were having keep them down, either.

"I'm glad I could help some people. I feel good about being in some way a part of their lives. Of course, I didn't make everyone happy—like some of the catchers in the Reds' minor league system." He also learned about the fickleness of the fans. He recalls a period in 1971 when he was being booed regularly by the hometown crowds. During one particular game, which his father was attending, Bench struck out twice and popped up in his first three times at bat. "The boos for me were rocking the stadium," recalls Bench. "My last time up, I got two strikes on me. Boo. Boo. Then I hit a home run to win the game. My dad jumped up and shouted, 'Boo now, you bums.' They didn't hear him. They were cheering."

Bench laughed. "But I have no complaints," he said. "I've gotten all the recognition anyone could dream for, and I've got financial security and helped my parents and went around the world and met all kinds of people. I've even been invited to the White House. That was 1969, and I met Mr. Nixon."

How had he felt about that? "Great," Bench said. "It was almost as good as meeting Willie Mays."

KOUFAX IS NO GARBO

July 3, 1985

WASHINGTON, D.C.—THERE WAS SOMETHING special about Sandy Koufax. On Monday night, in the Cracker Jack Old-Timers Baseball Classic at R.F. Kennedy Stadium here, he was chosen as the honorary captain of the National League team, a singular plum among such teammates as Henry Aaron and Ernie Banks and Warren Spahn. Koufax retains that special quality, apparently, even among his peers.

Perhaps it has something to do with an almost Biblical cycle to his baseball career. Koufax didn't quite have seven years thin and ill favored, and seven years of great plenty, but he did have six of each.

Miraculously, it seemed, he went from a pitcher of enormous but uncontrolled potential—catchers wore shin-guards when warming him up because so many of his pitches bounced in the dirt in front of them—to a star of the greatest mastery.

"What was it like facing Koufax? It was frightenin'," Banks, the former star Cub, recalled at the Cracker Jack, which the National League won, 7–3. "He had that tremendous fastball that would rise, and a great curveball that started at the eyes and broke to the ankles. In the end, you knew you were going to be embarrassed. You were either going to strike out or foul out."

Koufax's record was 36–40 in his first six seasons, 129–47 in his last six.

Maybe that special quality of Koufax also had to do with his poise and grit on the mound: the memory remains vivid of his breaking a World Series record in 1963 by striking out 15 Yankees in a game. Maybe the special quality also was enhanced by the air of distinction with which he comported himself, even to the way he adjusted his cap front and back, with two fingers of each hand, like knotting a bow tie.

And maybe the quality also had something to do with the way he retired, at the young age of 30, after having been named the Cy Young Award winner in 1966 for the third time in four years, after having led the major leagues in victories with 27, and earned-run average, 1.73, and games started and games completed and innings pitched and strikeouts, with 317, and after having helped pitch the Los Angeles Dodgers to a pennant, their second straight.

He suffered from an arthritic elbow, and doctors feared that if he continued pitching he could cause permanent damage to his arm.

And so, virtually at the height of his career, Koufax retired. And moved to a small town in Maine. Here was the toast of New York and Los Angeles departing the bright lights for what seemed to some the life of Greta Garbo.

To some, he became a kind of mystery man.

"What was so mysterious?" he asked, dressing for the game in the Cracker Jack clubhouse. "I wasn't running away, or hiding from the police. Maine is not another world. A lot of people lived there, and still do."

He said yes, he sought some privacy. "I never liked being shoved and pushed in crowds," he said. "But I was around for six years doing Saturday afternoon baseball telecasts with NBC.

"And now I work for the Dodgers. I'm a pitching coach with the team in spring training and a minor league pitching instructor during the summer months. I'm around. What's the mystery?"

Red Schoendienst came by. "Sandy," he said, "looks like you can go out there and still pump the heat."

Koufax smiled. At 6'0", 185 pounds, he does look fit. He was tan and slim and perhaps only the hair on his head, more salt than pepper now, gives an indication that on his next birthday, December 30, he will be 50 years old.

He spoke about traveling as a pitching instructor and working with young players. Bill Schweppe, the Dodgers' vice-president in charge of minor league operations, said that Koufax was effective with kids once they got past their awe of him. He mentioned Koufax's low-key approach that puts players at ease.

"In the minor leagues, the players are on the way up and they've all got their dreams," said Koufax. "It's a very positive thing. They want to learn. But I don't know how much I've helped anyone. I can show them some mechanics, but no one can make a big-league ballplayer. In the end it's up to the individual. They help themselves. But it's satisfying to see improvement."

He had said that he became a better pitcher when he learned to control his temper and his frustration. "Maybe it was just a matter of getting older," he said. "I see young players getting angry with themselves the way I did, and I wish I could tell them how to curb it. But there's no secret formula."

Koufax grew up in Brooklyn, joined the Dodgers there in 1955, at age 19, and never played a day in the minor leagues. "If I walked five guys in a major league game, it was terrible," he said, "but if I had done that in the minors, where I should have been, it would have been fine—a learning experience."

He contends that there was no single turning point. "I had a good spring in 1961," he said, "and it seemed that management was finally going to let me pitch every fourth day. Before, if I didn't do well in an outing, I might not pitch for three weeks. That didn't help me. I kept telling the Dodgers that I needed a routine. Your control is dependent on consistency."

In his younger, more inept days, a story goes that Koufax, who is Jewish, said he wasn't sure whether he was a *shlemiel* or a *shlamazel*. In Yiddish, a shlemiel is someone who spills soup on people, a shlamazel is someone who has soup spilled on him.

"Or is it vice versa?" Koufax said smiling. "I really don't remember if I ever said that, but there were times when I felt that way."

As he spoke, a television crew came by and began shooting him from the side. The bright light made him blink. He turned to the three men. "Don't television people ever ask?" he said, with a half smile.

"I'm sorry," said the man who apparently was head of the crew. He introduced himself. Koufax shook his hand, and said, "At least let me put on my shirt before you continue."

Later, he was asked if he still goes back to Maine. "Every year," he said. "I still love it."

PETE ROSE DESERVES TO BE IN THE HALL OF FAME

February 3, 2003

A CASE CAN BE made that Pete Rose will do virtually anything for money, including betting on baseball when he wore a major league uniform—"baseball's capital crime," as former commissioner Fay Vincent termed it. Today, at autograph signings and card shows, the career major league hits leader has his price, down to $165 for sardonically autographing the Dowd report, the explosive investigative analysis that was crucial to his lifetime banishment from Major League Baseball.

Now come published reports that Rose is gambling openly on sports in Las Vegas, just when the current baseball commissioner, Bud Selig, seemed to be leaning toward reinstating him if he could demonstrate that he has turned over a new nongambling leaf, admits his prior baseball transgressions, and adds an apology. Rose's sense of timing in this matter, unlike meeting a fastball with the fat of the bat, appears questionable.

John Dowd, the Washington lawyer and lead author of the report, added to newspaper accounts of Rose in Las Vegas by saying the other day that "a very reliable person told me that Rose was at the sports book in the Bellagio Hotel placing all kinds of bets on the Super Bowl." Dowd added, "This is hardly a way to reconfigure his life."

"Reconfigure his life" was the apt but arch phrase used by A. Bartlett Giamatti, then the baseball commissioner, when he terminated Rose's connection to baseball in 1989. Under baseball's rules, Rose was eligible to apply for reinstatement after a year.

The Dowd report is 225 pages and catalogs Rose's alleged baseball-related gambling, with an added seven volumes of 2,000 exhibits that present betting slips—some supposedly with Rose's fingerprints—numerous and suspicious phone calls to bookmakers or those connected to bookmakers, and other data.

While Rose, in all the years he has been persona non grata in baseball, has always denied he bet on baseball, he did admit to gambling on other sports and to attending racetracks. Millions of Americans participate in such activities, whether they do so in illegal or clandestine settings.

Some or all of this may have everything to do with Rose's being reinstated into baseball, which now prohibits him, for example, from managing a big-league team again or serving as a general manager, or a scout, or a peanut vendor.

But that is a separate issue from his being eligible for election to the Baseball Hall of Fame. He cannot be elected right now because the Hall of Fame's board of directors ruled in 1992—shortly before Rose was to become eligible—that anyone on baseball's ineligible list could not be admitted.

The contention here is that Rose ought to be given a chance to be elected to the Hall of Fame. If the gambling issue hadn't arisen, he would have been a near-unanimous selection.

There has never been an accusation that Pete Rose, nicknamed Charlie Hustle because of his desire to succeed on the baseball field, ever threw a game as a player or played less than his best. All of the exhibits in the Dowd report go from 1987 to 1989, when Rose was strictly the field manager of the Cincinnati Reds.

Rose was player-manager of the Reds from 1984 through 1986. No hard evidence in the Dowd report alleges that Rose gambled on baseball as a player or a player-manager. "The only evidence is according to witnesses," Dowd said. There were three primary "witnesses" who were connected themselves to illegal gambling with Rose in one form or another. Witnesses, as any lawyer can tell you, may or may not be reliable, depending, perhaps, on their own agendas.

If Pete Rose were to be eligible for election to the Hall of Fame, it would not be for managing, but for performance as a player.

There are those who insist that Rose make a full confession before gaining eligibility to the Hall. This is contradictory reasoning. Even if he did confess to gambling on baseball, that would not change the fact that he gambled on baseball, and not change his having committed baseball's capital crime. With that logic, he should never be named to the Hall of Fame, period.

Either he deserves to be in the Hall of Fame for his great 24-year playing career in the major leagues, or he doesn't. If the character issue were used broadly, numerous drunks, womanizers, racists, convicted tax evaders, and drug users now immortalized with plaques in the Hall would be thrown out. There is strong, documented evidence that even Ty Cobb and Tris Speaker, two all-time greats, conspired to fix a game.

There are Hall of Famers, like Bob Feller and Ralph Kiner, who are adamant, at this time at least, against Rose being made eligible for the Hall. There are others, like Mike Schmidt, Rose's teammate on the Phillies for five years, including two World Series teams, who hold the opposing view. In his Hall of Fame acceptance speech in 1995, Schmidt said he joined "millions of baseball fans around the world in hoping that someday soon, someday very soon, Pete Rose will be standing right here." He added, "Pete stood for winning, we all know that."

Rose remains hugely popular among many fans. When the All-Century team was announced in Atlanta at the World Series in 1999, Rose got the greatest round of applause, greater even than the hometown hero Hank Aaron. When the Greatest Moments in Baseball nominees were presented at last year's World Series in Pac Bell Park in San Francisco, Rose, a finalist for his hit that broke Cobb's record of 4,191 hits, received the loudest and longest ovation.

"It's amazing," said Marty Brennaman, the Reds' play-by-play announcer, "but Pete remains so popular in Cincinnati that if he ran for mayor, he'd be elected in a landslide."

The Hall of Fame pitcher Robin Roberts, in New York yesterday to receive an achievement award at the New York Baseball Writers dinner, considered such responses to Rose. "People like the underdog," he said.

They like the underdog when they believe the dog has been treated unfairly. And a Rose by any other name fits that distinction, as well as deserving a plaque in the Baseball Hall of Fame.

ROBERTO CLEMENTE'S PRESENCE STILL FELT

March 16, 1973

BRADENTON, FLORIDA—ROBERTO CLEMENTE WOULD sometimes remind his wife, Vera, "If anything ever happens to me, do not kill yourself. You must care for our little babies."

Mrs. Clemente told this to Manny Sanguillen while he was staying at the Clemente house for two weeks in January and helping in the search for Clemente's still unrecovered body. Clemente, as the world knows, was killed in a plane crash last New Year's Eve one mile off the shore of San Juan, Puerto Rico, attempting to fly relief supplies to earthquake victims in Nicaragua.

Sanguillen, possibly Clemente's best friend on the Pirates, recalled that Vera was trying to "take everything," the way Roberto had. "He used to tell her that she knew how much trouble he had to go through to get where he did. That when he first came to spring training in Florida, how much he had to fight because he was a black guy, and because he was Puerto Rican," said Sanguillen.

"And you know Vera is Roberto Clemente's wife, the wife of a superstar, because she has the same kind of pride and dignity he had."

"But," said Sanguillan recently at the Pittsburgh training site here, "no matter how hard she try, every time she sees me, she cries.

"She remembers to me how we used to kid. Like the time she was waiting at the Pittsburgh airport when we returned from a road trip. I decided to limp, to kid her. She saw me and said, 'Oh, Sangy, what happen?' And Roberto say, 'Vera, don't listen to that crazy Panamanian.'"

When Sanguillen came to the Clemente home after the tragedy, he was anxious to see how the three Clemente children, Roberto Jr., eight, Luis, seven, and Enrique, four, were getting along.

"Ricky, the youngest one, ran to me when he saw me," said Sanguillen. "Then he put his head down and he say, 'Daddy gone.' Both the boys would play cowboys, and they are okay, I can see."

It is tougher for the mother, said Sanguillen. No body has yet been found. The Coast Guard found a briefcase which was identified as Clemente's. And Vera herself discovered one brown sock washed onto the beach; she says Roberto was wearing that sock the night of the flight.

"She knows he is dead," said Sanguillen, "but every night she waits for him to come home."

Clemente is alive in a way for Sanguillen, too. "His spirit is with me," he said. "I dream of him." In an odd set of circumstances, Sanguillen, Pittsburgh's regular catcher since 1969, is one of several players who are being tested for right field, Clemente's position. Sanguillen in right would give Milt May, a fine prospect but bench-warmer for the last two seasons, a chance to catch.

Strangely, Sanguillen had been tried in the outfield briefly last season and this winter played a little right field for the team Clemente managed in San Juan in the Winter League.

"Deep inside I don't have the heart to take Roberto's place," said Sanguillen. "He is gone, he has all the best records in baseball. Nobody can match him. But I just feel he is with me in right field. His spirit is there, giving me tips like he always did, ever since I came up to the big leagues in 1969. He say he help me because I have to potential to be a superstar. But he help everybody."

Now Sanguillen, who like all the Pirates wears a black ribbon on the left sleeve of his uniform in memory of Clemente, smiled; his is a frequent, generous, round-faced, gap-toothed smile which makes him resemble a chocolate pumpkin.

"It is good to know Roberto was happy in his last years," said Sanguillen. "He carry this team, he and Bill Mazeroski, for 17, 18 years. He tell me, 'Sangy, I am happy man. We are winning. For years I could not sleep nights because we are losing.' And then he got his 3,000th big-league hit at the end of last season. Exactly 3,000. And in 1971 he had the greatest World Series anyone ever had. He showed the world how great he was. But we all knew, all the Pirates.

"Like one time last year Don Money of the Phillies was rounding third on a base hit to Clemente. Clemente faked like he was fumbling the ball. Money tried to make it home. But a perfect throw got him. It was a tough play, though, because I had to block the plate hard. When Clemente come in from right, I ask him, 'Did you fumble on purpose to make Money run?' He said yes. I said, 'Okay, you know *you* can make a perfect throw in time to get him. But how you know *I* can hold on to the ball?'

"He said, 'Because I have confidence in you.' I said, 'Bob—you terrific.'"

BROOKS ROBINSON: SUPER PLAYMAKER

October 12, 1970

BALTIMORE—THE PLAY BROOKS ROBINSON made in the sixth inning of the first 1970 World Series game should be a tireless topic of admiration this winter around pot-bellied hot stoves, or wherever it is that modern America now sits and warms its memories.

Clay Carroll, Cincinnati relief pitcher, will remember it this way: "He was going toward the bullpen when he threw to first. His arm went one way, his body another, and his shoes another."

Baltimore Oriole manager Earl Weaver will have the play jumbled in a mental collection of superior Brooks Robinson plays.

"So Brooks Robinson made another great play," said Weaver after that first game, maintaining a straight face. "So what?"

"Watch him day in and day out and he'll do something unbelievable around third base every day," added Weaver, perhaps suppressing a yawn. "No, the amazing is nothing new when it comes to Brooksie."

But Robinson, 33 and baldish, is not so blasé. "It was one of my better ones, I'll tell you that," he said. That covers a lot of ground. It covers all the territory around third base that any normal, red-blooded superman could cover in 15 major league seasons. For the last 10 consecutive years, he has earned the Gold Glove Award for excellence at his position.

To describe that play is as easy as bottling a rainbow. But the primary colors were: sixth inning. Cincinnati power hitter Lee May up. Robinson playing about 20 feet behind third base and some 10 feet in from the foul line. May hits medium-hard bouncer down the line.

"He hit a nice, a nice...," began Robinson, trying to give details of the play in the locker room afterward.

"A nice double?" interjected a reported.

Robinson's blue eyes laughed above the swatches of charcoal on his cheek bones. "No, if it were a stinger, I mean a real B-B shot, then I'd never have gotten it."

In his strangely heavy-legged manner, his head all aflop, he impossibly backhanded his glove in the path of the ball. He was now in foul territory.

"In the 1966 series," he said, "I didn't get but three or four routine balls. But you're known as a good fielder and you'd like to prove it. That's what it's all about, isn't it? Last year's series I made two hard plays in the first two games and I was happy to show that.

"Sure, you think about all the people watching in the stands and the millions and millions watching on television.

"I'll stand at third base waiting for the pitch and I'll think about that. I remember late this season we were on a nationally televised Monday night game in Boston. That afternoon my parents called from home in Little Rock. It was their 35th wedding anniversary. My mom said they'd be watching. 'You do good, son,' she told me. I went 0-for-5, struck out twice, and made two errors..."

It seemed somehow that Robinson was throwing to first base even before the ball had stopped bouncing. He threw "over the top," that is, not sidearm, and the ball bounced one time and plopped into Boog Powell's glove and beat May by half a step or so.

"I didn't have time to aim it," said Robinson. "I just saw everybody over there and kinda let it go. I have pretty good balance and I'm fortunate to be able to throw from almost any position. I'm not too fast—I'll never have to worry about slowing down—but my reflexes and timing's good. And my arm's not the strongest, but I can get the ball away fast.

"I do wish the ball would've got to first on a fly. But I couldn't put enough on it."

To a perfectionist, even the most perfect of performances can be improved upon in retrospect. But how do you make the blue in the rainbow deeper?

Ironically, it was another player's great defensive play off a Brooks Robinson line drive that the year before conceivably turned the 1969 World Series for the Mets. With the Mets leading Baltimore 1–0 in the ninth inning of Game 4 (the Mets ahead in the Series 3 games to 1), Ron Swoboda made a spectacular diving catch of Robinson's sinking line drive. While the trying run scored from third, it seemingly ended an Oriole rally. The Mets, with Tom Seaver going the distance, won the game in the 10th inning, 2–1. The Mets went on to take the Series 4 games to 1.

BOB GIBSON'S WORLD

June 30, 1969

"(On the playing field, the athlete) presents himself naked before the world.... The athlete shows us what we ideally are as bodies.... The world's impersonal process has him as a focal point.

"It is because he is an outstanding instance of what man might do and be that an athlete is an outstanding man.... Athletes are excellence in the guise of men.

"(But) sooner or later the athlete falls short. Eventually he reveals some failure of nerve, self-discipline, courage, insight, generosity, caution, or imagination. These limitations we treat somewhat in the way we deal with those that characterize thinkers, artists, and religious men. We tend to blame the failures on the individual, not on the man...."

From *Sport: A Philosophic Inquiry* by Dr. Paul Weiss

THE LOCKER ROOM IS a comfortable place, not so much physically—what with the stools and simple steel lockers—but mentally. The athlete is alone there with his peers, not having to prove his worth over and over again. As he does on the field before crowds.

"I don't like crowds, and fans, except for a very few; are all fair-weather," said St. Louis Cardinal pitcher Bob Gibson, suiting up in the sanctity of the clubhouse.

"People think they own you because you're a famous athlete. And that's horse manure. They treat you as an object rather than a human being. My job is to give 100 percent on the field. Off the field, I should be left alone to be a private man. People just don't see it that way.

"Day in and day out people are coming to me and asking me to do things, talk to them, sign autographs, pose for pictures. And they don't care what you're doing at the time.

"Not long ago I was eating in a restaurant. A woman comes over and asks for an autograph. I told her politely that if she left the paper I would sign it when I was finished eating. She went back, told her husband. He came over and said, 'You think you're too big to sign an autograph?' He tore up the paper and threw it in my face.

"I'm not the type of guy who can turn the other cheek. I waited about five minuets to cool off. Then I went to their table and gave him a piece of my mind. Another time I was sitting on a plane with my wife and some guy comes over and says, 'You're Bob Gibson, aren't you?' I said yes. He said, 'Go to Hell.'

"Recently, my two daughters asked me to take them on the pleasure boat *Huck Finn* for a ride down the Mississippi in St Louis. I hesitated because I knew what would happen. Well, I hadn't seen them in two months, so I said okay. I wore sunglasses and hid my head between my legs. But pretty soon nearly everyone on that boat—must've been 300 people—were around me. I refused to sign any autographs. And I know they went away saying, 'Bob Gibson, that creep.'

"You get callous treatment on the field, too. I'll never forget something that happened two years ago. I had been on a winning streak. Then one game I got bombed for nine runs in about 10 minutes. I was terrible. We didn't even have time for anyone to warm up. As I came off the field, I was booed. And this from the St. Louis fans who are usually good as fans go. The next day I got a bunch of mail from fans apologizing for the others.

"What I like about my job is that I don't hear the crowd. When I'm on the mound it's just me and the batter. But I almost never pay attention to cheers—sure, I like that—or boos. If I had my choice, though, I'd rather pitch before empty stands.

"Mail is interesting, too. During the World Series a Washington sportswriter saw me reading the mail and asked to look at it. There were hate letters, about my being outspoken on race matters. He printed the letter. I got 3,000 letters apologizing for that one. It took me all winter to read through them. I appreciated that.

"Even though I am outspoken about race, I still feel no obligation to black people or to kids or anyone else. But it's funny. I bought a house in a previously all-white neighborhood in Omaha and some blacks even criticized me for that.

"I do think it's good for kids to have idols, someone to look up to, someone who has achieved a goal. I didn't have someone who represented a goal. I waited until Jackie Robinson got into baseball. All blacks had in those days was Stepin Fetchit, the movie clown. And I remember he embarrassed me, sitting right there in the theatre, because he was making a fool of himself and others were making a fool of him. Our futures looked dim. So we'd say, 'Well, let's go out and rob a bank.'

"Now I'm a hero of sorts. But the day will come when people turn away from me. They'll grab onto someone else. That's the way people are. I won't be disappointed or bitter. Maybe I'll even be a little relieved."

LOU BROCK STEALS PAST FATHER TIME

September 13, 1978

YOU KNEW SOMETHING TERRIFIC would happen the minute Lou Brock of the St. Louis Cardinals reached first base.

He'd take a lead off the bag, cool as could be. The pitcher'd fuss around, peer over his shoulder, step off the rubber, flip quickly to first to keep Brock close.

Heavy with paraphernalia, the catcher would lumber out to the mound for a heart-to-heart.

The crowd picked up the tension and began to chant, "Lou... Lou...Lou." For this was the base-stealing champ of baseball on first base, and now the whole joint was jumpin'. He rarely disappointed.

In 1974, Lou Brock stole 118 bases to break Maury Wills' single-season record. Brock led the National League in stolen bases in eight seasons. In September of last year, he swiped the 893rd of his career and passed Ty Cobb's 50-year mark. They had a parade down the main drag of St. Louis for him after that.

Now it all seems in the dim, dusty past. Lou is slowing down. He's 39 years old and in his 17th full big-league season. Although he's a career .294 batter, in the steamy dog days of this summer he was breaking his back to get above .200. By early September, he edged past .220.

It materially affects his base-stealing. He had only 17 thefts by early September. Well, you can't steal first base, goes the cruel baseball cliché.

Brock spends many games on the cushioned dugout bench. An article in a magazine mentions in passing "...the seldom-seen Brock." When he does start games, he is sometimes called back as he heads to the plate and a pinch hitter is announced for him.

"Yes," he admits, "it is humiliating."

"No question about it—Brock is finished." Brock heard this report over the radio one day. It did not fill him with joy.

He is sitting now perched on a railing in the long runway between clubhouse and playing field in the dark, cool, steel cavern of the stadium. He remains lean, though his face seems rounder than in the past, and perhaps it's just the light from the weak yellow bulb overhead but Brock's eyes seem particularly soft and moist as he talks about these tough times.

He repeatedly bounces a baseball absently onto the concrete runway and snatches it with his red lefty's glove.

"I still think I've got at least one good solid year left," he says. "All this happened so suddenly. Last season management came to me and said they were going to platoon me in left field. They said they wanted to give some of the younger guys a shot. The club was going bad and they had to look to the future. But hell, here I am coming off a .300 season and 56 stolen bases.

"They just saw age. Thirty-eight. That's *all* they saw. Well, a lot of uncertainty crept in for me. It affected my play.

"Before, I'd come to the park mentally prepared to play, having thought about how I'd handle the pitcher...the catcher."

Brock claims he could steal a base before the game even began. He'd capture the eye of the rival catcher during batting practice. Brock would glare at him. At the plate Brock waited until the catcher crouched, then he'd turn and look *down* at him.

"A part-time player can't very well carry that off," said Brock.

He bounced the ball, caught it.

"You know, I've never seen a guy who left the game gracefully," continued Brock. "All of us old guys always think we've got one more good year left. Some do. Look at Pete Rose and the season he's having and he's 37." Brock smiled. "Pete gave the over-35 guys hope."

Brock will return in 1979. He has a $200,000-a-year contract. "I really do think I could contribute to making this club a contender again, otherwise I wouldn't come back," he said. Also, he needs a little more than 100 hits to join the exclusive 3,000-hit club.

The baseball bounced and echoed in the cavern. Brock had a faraway look now, and in the solitude of the dark runway he may have been dreamily recalling another echo—a driving, thrilling echo: "Lou...Lou...Lou."

HENRY AARON: BASEBALL STAR AS BLACK ACTIVIST

August 13, 1975

ATLANTA—WHAT DOES THAT RECORD, THE record, mean to Henry Aaron, the man who most assuredly will break it?

"It means," he says, sitting in a sawed-off blue sweatshirt before his locker cubicle, "that people listen to me now where, say, 10 years ago, my words got lost."

Only in the last two years has Aaron begun to receive the national recognition that his phenomenal career has so richly deserved. Only, that is, since his pursuit of the career home run record held by babe Ruth has brought him inescapably, finally, into the limelight.

People listen to him because they are watching him. And it becomes of great interest to know what kind of man he is. He also is greatly aware of this: "Ruth's record is about the last thing in professional sports that whites can hang onto—the legendary record of the Sultan of Swat," he says.

He has recently become identified with black causes. For example, he is now a close personal friend of the Reverend Jesse Jackson, a leading young black spokesman. Aaron, in winter, now is the organizer of a celebrity bowling tournament in Atlanta with proceeds going to research on sickle cell anemia, a disease that afflicts black people disproportionately.

Aaron is also outspoken on the progress, or lack of it, for blacks in baseball. He says that blacks are stagnating. "Whatever so-called progress there is—like blacks staying in the same hotels with the white players—this came about from civil rights legislation, not from any leveling action by baseball," says Aaron.

"Why aren't there no black managers? Why aren't there even no black third-base coaches? There are token first-base coaches—a few. But what does a first-base coach do? He has no duties. No responsibilities. Nothing. Absolutely nothing. He's not expected to have any intelligence."

Aaron still feels some of the clichés of being black. He remembers that once blacks were considered "too gutless" to be able to take the pressures of day-in, day-out major league baseball.

"Jackie Robinson changed a lot of those beliefs," says Aaron. "His courage and intelligence showed what the black man could be made out of.

"I hear about blacks having natural ability, natural rhythm. That's not the only reason for the blacks' success in baseball, or in sports. Look at Maury Wills. It takes a lot of thought, a lot of analyzing to steal 104 bases in a season.

"And you don't hit over 700 home runs in a career by just having natural rhythm. You need discipline. You study the pitchers. I'm sure I know the National League pitchers as well as Ted Williams knew the American League pitchers when he batted .400."

Aaron's hero off the field is Dr. Martin Luther King. "He could walk with kings and talk with presidents," said Aaron. "He wasn't for lootings and bombings and fights but he wasn't afraid of violence, either. He was 20 years ahead of his times."

King's death by assassination cannot, of course, be forgotten by Aaron. Sometimes Aaron wonders about that, too. He says that among the hundreds of letters he receives weekly, many are threats on his life.

"But I can't think about that," he says. "If I'm a target, then I'm a target. I can only worry about doing my job, and doing it good."

Aaron believes that Ruth's record should be broken, just as it should someday be broken if he becomes the holder.

"I think it's good for all America," he said. "The world keeps going on. Kids today can relate to me. And besides, why should they relate to a ballplayer who quit playing 35 years ago?

"I think it also gives black kids hope. It shows them that anything is possible today. Maybe they can't be a ballplayer like me, but they can strive for excellence, and be a good doctor or lawyer or anything. I believe that I would have tried to be the best at whatever I did, even if it was being a dirt-shoveler."

It wasn't that way for Aaron when he was a boy. He was the third child in a family of eight children in Mobile, Alabama. His father was a rivet-bucker. Aaron played baseball but he had no hopes of making the game a career.

"There were no blacks in Major League Baseball until I was 13 or 14, and Jackie Robinson broke in in 1947," said Aaron. "He gave us all hope."

Aaron was asked about the coincidence that Babe Ruth died just one year later. Did his death at the time mean anything to Aaron?

"No, not really," said Aaron. "Ruth was in a different world. Baseball when he played was something no black kid could relate to. We had nothing to wish for. You know, of all the pictures I've ever seen of Babe Ruth, I've never seen one with him and black kids. Have you? This is no knock on Ruth. It's just the way it was. I don't think many blacks want to the baseball games. It's like I don't go to ice hockey games, even though it might be a great sport. But I can't relate because there are no blacks in that game."

It was Robinson who allowed Aaron to "relate" to baseball. Aaron holds immense respect and gratitude for Robinson and his memory.

"Before Jackie died, in the days when he was going blind," said Aaron, "we had long talks. I will never forget that he told me to keep talking about what makes me unhappy, to keep the pressure on. Otherwise, people will think you're satisfied with the situation."

MARGE SCHOTT, LONER OWNER

June 12, 1996

IT SEEMS CERTAIN THAT Marge Schott will be forced to decide today whether to relinquish control of her ballclub, the Cincinnati Reds, or suffer a suspension again, for a one- or two-year sentence.

It is certain that Marge Schott embarrasses her fellow owners by her insensitive, boorish and bigoted remarks.

Bud Selig, a fellow owner with the conflict-of-interest title of acting commissioner, said earlier this week, "Yes, she has hurt baseball, no question about it."

If ever someone has advertised her ignorance it is the baseball team owner Marge Schott. She is on record of making slurs toward blacks, Jews, working women, Italians, Asians—and these are only the ethnic and racial groups that she was asked about.

As far back as 1992, she remarked to me that "Hitler was good in the beginning, but he went too far." That was one of the particulars in the indictment that got her suspended from baseball for a year in 1993.

When on opening day this season in Cincinnati, the umpire John McSherry collapsed and died on the field in the first inning, and the game was canceled, she complained, "First it was snow, and now this!" It was as if she believed God was conspiring against her having a decent opening day.

And when she sent the umpires flowers in an attempt to make up, the flowers were discovered to have been recycled. A television station had sent them to her the day before.

Many people who know her describe her as a lonely widow, without children, and with a drinking problem. All this may be true. But in my time spent with Marge Schott, I have found her to be a person of firm convictions and with a pittance of information. She knew as little about Hitler, for example, as she did the infield fly rule.

As for her drinking: when she made that Hitler remark to me, it was 10:00 in the morning, she was driving a car and driving it straight, under the influence of nothing but her simple, unworldly, minimally educated self.

She does, however, appear to have a quirky if not crafty business sense.

Her fellow owners will tell you that she knows nothing about how to run an organization. But if people are so set against her, then they would not, or should not, show up to her team's games. But they do. Last season, in the smallest metropolitan market of the 14 National League teams, the Reds had a home attendance of 1.8 million fans and outdrew eight of Schott's competitors, including the New York Mets, by 500,000.

Her fellow owners will tell you that she knows nothing about baseball. But in the 11 full seasons she has owned the Reds, they have been winners. And in the 1990s, only the Atlanta Braves have a better on-the-field record than the Reds.

And while the Reds are in last place this season and playing only .400 ball, they won their division last year—the same twist experienced by the Boston Red Sox.

Schott has the lowest ticket prices in all of baseball and has insisted on fans being able to buy a hot dog at Riverfront Stadium for a dollar. An organization in Chicago called the Fan Cost Index figured out that for a family of four to attend a ballgame—from tickets to parking to popcorn—the Reds have the lowest total average cost: $81.31. The average is $102.58, with the Yankees coming in at $117.32 and the Mets at $104.80.

As for hurting baseball, what hurt baseball more than the owners calling off the World Series in 1994? What hurt them more financially than the $280 million they had to pay the players for illegally colluding to hold down salaries? And not one owner had to relinquish control of his club, or was suspended for it, either.

And just who are these fellow owners sitting in judgment of her? The admitted felon in the Bronx? Ted Turner of Atlanta, who urinated in public after his America's Cup yacht racing victory?

The owners would distinguish themselves not by taking club control away from Schott, or by suspending her, but by saying that while her speech and actions are despicable, it is also true that in America everyone has a right to make a fool of oneself.

It is the right of the customers, however, not to patronize such a fool. So far, the fans in Cincinnati and in the National League cities have not seen fit to send that message. But they should be the ultimate judges, not her pious fellow owners.

• • •

Under threat of another suspension by baseball's executive council, Marge Schott was forced to give up the daily operation of the Reds. She was never again a significant presence in baseball. She died in 2004 at age 75.

PAUL O'NEILL MOVES ON GRACEFULLY

November 7, 2001

THE TALL MAN WITH the familiar gentle face, his eight-year-old son at his side, entered Yankee Stadium for the last time yesterday morning as a member of the Yankees. He happened to glance ahead, and through the tunnel he noticed a piecemeal view of the park. How bright the green grass looked in the sunshine, he thought, how beautiful.

He allowed himself now a pang of nostalgia—not regret, but a sweet remembrance of things past, of the excitement of games and pennant races that never paled for him. He had rarely taken notice of this sight through all these years when hurrying from the players' entrance to the locker room, but on this day, this bittersweet ending, he paused.

Paul O'Neill had come back to the Stadium to pack up the contents of his locker. He will not be back. After 21 years as a professional baseball player, 17 years in the majors, the last nine as a Yankee, the man many consider—pardon the platitude—the heart and soul of championship teams (five World Series appearances with the Yankees) and championship attitudes, as well as right fielder exemplar and left-handed clutch hitter in the middle of the lineup, is retiring, at age 38.

"Feels strange," he said, in sweatshirt and jeans, as, with a little help from his son, Aaron, he placed items into a large cardboard box that will be sent to his home in Cincinnati. "I've never cleaned out my locker before. I mean, everything. And I didn't work out today. Usually, right after the last game, you go back to working out, preparing for next season."

Paul O'Neill, who led the Yankees with a .333 batting average in this Series—and did the same in the World Series the year before when he hit .474 against the Mets—remained in many ways the symbol of the Yankees who, whether they liked it or not, whether it truly applied or not, came to symbolize for multitudes the grit of the city as it attempted to pull itself up from of the unspeakable attack on September 11.

They had come from behind to win games in stunning fashion. Then they lost the last game of the season, the postseason, in stunning fashion. The team had flown back from Phoenix after the less-than-agreeable conclusion of the World Series Sunday night. Would he come back for an old-timers' game?

"The way I ran to third Sunday," he said, "I already did." This was a joke about his having been thrown out at third in the first inning after hitting a ball into the right-center-field gap. What he didn't say was, Arizona had to make a perfect relay to get him, but he still set a tone for aggressive and intelligent play.

Baseball, though, wasn't as pleasurable as it once was for O'Neill because, he said, "this hurts, that hurts." "I wasn't as productive as I once was," he said. So O'Neill had decided before this season that this would be his last, but didn't emphasize it because, typically, he didn't want the attention.

But playing baseball games could still be thrilling. "When I first came up to the majors, in September of '85, with Cincinnati," he said, "I wondered how guys like Rose and Concepcion and Perez could be so cool about playing, while I was shaking in my boots. But, you know, I always got butterflies before games, my whole career, and was happy I did. The adrenalin was always there, the excitement was always there."

He said he had been dubious about coming to New York, in 1993, when traded from Cincinnati. "I came here not knowing what street the Empire State Building was on, and I became a part of the community, and it was where my three children were born," he said. "It was the best nine or 10 years of my life."

Like most Yankees, he was uncomfortable with having the team looked at as a symbol in these tragic times. "If we gave joy to people, and helped in a small way to unify the city, that's wonderful," he said. "But for me, there are two different stories—there was life and death, and there were baseball games."

His future? Spend time with his family, maybe do some baseball broadcasting. Few, however, will forget the warm, appreciative chants of "Paul-ie, Paul-ie," that rose from the 56,000 fans crammed into Yankee Stadium in his last home game, Game 5 of the World Series, last Thursday night. It is guessed that rightly his number, 21, will be retired by the Yankees.

As for the Yankees in this Series, "Sure, it was disappointing to lose, especially with a close game in Game 7," he said, "but it was Arizona's time. We did all we could. Don't think anyone could do anything more."

Which mirrors precisely what Paul O'Neill has done and meant for the Yankees, their fans, and the City of New York.

JIM ABBOTT'S INSPIRATIONAL RETURN

May 21, 1999

SOME PEOPLE MAY SURELY be surprised to see Jim Abbott back on a major league mound, after what happened last year, or the year before, and, to be sure, the year before that. Even the first part of this season.

But Jim Abbott has always been full of surprises, including making the major leagues at all, the only pitcher known to have reached the big time with just one hand.

Yet here was the 6'3", 210-pound left-hander for the Milwaukee Brewers getting ready to face the Mets' lineup in the first game of a doubleheader at Shea Stadium yesterday, with a dispiriting 0–4 record and lugging around an 8.49 earned-run average.

This was his first start in three weeks, after having been relegated to the bullpen after three unimpressive starts. He didn't complain of the demotion to manager Phil Garner. "How could I?" Abbott said. "I didn't have a leg to stand on."

Garner was sorry to drop the invariably polite, diligent Abbott from the rotation. "You hope he finds himself," Garner said. "He's a gutsy guy, and maybe the harder he tries the less effective he is. He's no longer a power pitcher, but more of a finesse pitcher, and he's in the transition of trying to master it. I just want him to throw free and easy."

Garner is giving him another shot as a starter, and Abbott knows he either succeeds now, or may very soon run out the string here.

Abbott has had some wonderful accomplishments in his 10 big-league seasons, including an 18–11 year with the Angels in 1991 and a no-hitter for the Yankees in 1993. But he fell on rocky times in Gotham and was traded to the Angels. Three seasons ago he won two games and lost 18, and was released by Anaheim. "I felt," he said, "uneasy with myself."

And he quit the game, at 29. He had rarely quit at anything, always determined to forge ahead. When he was five years old, in Flint, Michigan, his parents had fitted him with a hook for a hand. He came back from kindergarten crying that the other kids had made fun of him and were afraid to play with him. He removed the hook, never to wear it again.

He endeavored to prove himself in myriad ways, none more dramatically than on the athletic field, becoming a baseball star at the University of Michigan and going straight into the major leagues.

He inevitably became a hero and model to many who felt disadvantaged.

"I don't carry that as a burden," he said. "I've looked at my life as a personal journey. But I'd say in 50 percent of the parks we play in, parents of kids with one hand, or some other disability, bring their kids to meet me."

And sometimes, as he did in Pittsburgh recently, he will play catch with them on the sidelines, removing their gloves to throw.

"It's the quietest kids that move me the most," he recalled. "You see their shyness, that they want to be like everybody else. I understand that. And they open up a little bit. It's inspiring."

After he quit baseball he sat around his home in Michigan watching baseball games on television—he was still being paid around $3 million from his Angels contract—and realizing that it was still very much in his blood. After that season of inactivity, his agent called the White Sox and Abbott last season returned to, of all places, Hickory, North Carolina, Class A ball.

He was moved him up to Class AA, then Class AAA, and, finally, last September, to the White Sox, for whom he was a remarkable 5–0 in that last month of the season. He became a free agent and signed a one-year contract with Milwaukee for $400,000 plus bonuses.

The game yesterday began forlornly for Abbott, and ended that way. Robin Ventura belted a bases-loaded home run off him in the first inning. His throwing error in the fourth cost him a run. In the bottom of the fifth, he gave up two hits with one out, and Garner removed him. The next batter homered, and Abbott, who was credited with giving up seven runs on seven hits in 4⅓ innings and was the losing pitcher, could hardly have been a bundle of joy as he soaped himself in the shower, and contemplated his future, at 0–5.

"He obviously didn't do very well today," Garner said. "But right now he's still in the rotation."

In spring training, when Abbott was throwing well and looking like a star again, and hitting a single and laying down a sacrifice bunt, since National League pitchers must bat, Mark McGwire said it best.

"If Jim Abbott doesn't inspire you," McGwire said, "there's something wrong with you."

Nothing, really, has changed.

V.

WHY BASEBALL AT ALL

EAGER TO SEE THE RETURN OF PEANUTS AND CRACKER JACK

October 11, 2001

I WANT TO MISS "Take Me Out to the Ball Game." I want to miss the inanity of it, of the peanuts and the Cracker Jack and not caring if I never get back. And I indeed miss the time, a lifetime ago, a hundred thousand years ago, it seems, in a world now so utterly unrecognizable, so relatively benign, that we could indeed forget our problems for three hours at a ballpark.

Now, at the seventh-inning stretch in baseball games, instead of the traditional "Take Me Out to the Ball Game," they are playing "God Bless America."

I like "God Bless America," too. And I've been in ballparks in the last few weeks in which they've played it. I've stood, with the rest of the fans, and the ballplayers, who come out and stand in front of the dugouts and appear to be singing their hearts out like the others while facing the fluttering American flag.

It is moving. The game stops dead in its tracks, and we remember the atrocities committed at the World Trade Center and at the Pentagon, and the battle in the plane that crashed in Pennsylvania, as well as the bravery and goodness of so many in response.

But I miss that sweet song, "Take Me Out to the Ball Game," that ode to triviality.

"God Bless America" halts the dream world to recall the nightmare.

It is so because we cannot really forget what is so fresh a blow, regardless of how well Schilling is pitching or Bonds is hitting, or how Ripken and Gwynn are lavishly celebrated at career's end.

I hope the new seventh-inning song doesn't last past these playoffs and the World Series. I hope we've had enough of what the song means to us at so raw a time that we won't need to be reminded of it again, or as often. It would mean returning, partially anyway, to a world we once knew. It would mean staving off threats from enemies. It will be difficult. I know a woman who bought a gas mask for herself, her husband, and her two dogs, anticipating germ warfare here. She is a baseball fan, but the games have lost their luster for her.

I know a New Jersey man who gave up his tickets to the opening Knicks game in which they play host to the Washington Wizards on October 30, which will be Michael Jordan's first regular season game since his last retirement. Instead, the man is going to the comparatively quiet Nets opener in the Meadowlands the same night. He said that out of fear of terrorists he now won't have to go into Penn Station or through the Lincoln Tunnel or over the George Washington Bridge, or be in Madison Square Garden for this "hyped-up" event.

I know someone else, a season ticket holder to Yankee games, who has given up his postseason tickets because he wants to stay home where he can have split screens: the Yankees, and CNN for breaking news.

But people are showing up to the games despite the anxieties, despite the fears. Yet you wonder if anyone could now truly sing "Take Me Out to the Ball Game" with the genial devotion it once took, after passing through heavy security at the gate and observing German shepherds, held on the leashes by police officers, sniffing the premises for bombs.

The singing of "The Star Spangled Banner" at sporting events was first documented at the 1918 World Series, when the United States was involved in World War I. It was the Chicago Cubs against the Boston Red Sox, and Babe Ruth pitched a 1–0 six-hitter before only 19,274 fans in Comiskey Park. The Cubs had moved across town from their smaller ballpark, now known as Wrigley Field, to seek greater attendance at a larger park. But the stadium was less than half-filled, demonstrating that, like today, many fans' minds were elsewhere.

The singing of the national anthem may have waned after the war, but it returned full force and forever more after Pearl Harbor.

Ballgames were stopped for a week or so after September 11 out of respect for those who died, as well as the fact that few had the desire to play or watch games. We've returned, seeking to live and play again as before, to a degree anyway. I'm reminded that during World War II, President Roosevelt insisted that the games should go on because they were vital to the country's morale.

"If need be," Red Smith wrote at the time, "we could get along without baseball for a while. We can get along without cuffs on our pants, without pleasure cars, without plumbing or central heat. But we are not yet ready to admit that the Axis can make us give up all these things, even temporarily."

So we go to the pleasure domes that are our playgrounds, and, unable yet to suspend disbelief, we sing with often moist eyes not "Take Me Out to the Ball Game" but "God Bless America."

It's what we need for now. After all, it's still letting us, with raised voices, "root, root, root for the home team."

THE SPARKLE OF THE DIAMOND

June 24, 1986

PUT YOURSELF IN BO Jackson's shoes. How could you not choose baseball over football? In this case, the outfield in the Kansas City Royals organization over the backfield for the Tampa Bay Buccaneers.

Baseball is a pleasant pastime, a genial undertaking, a civil essay. Football is war.

Baseball is a kid's game. You put on a beanie and knickers to play it. In football, you don armor.

When you put on a baseball cap, it shields the sun. When you tug on a football helmet, it burns your ears.

When it rains in baseball, you seek shelter. People usually have the good sense to go indoors and eat hot dogs. In football, people sit outside in thunderstorms, in lightning, in snow and sleet. Of course, they must come equipped with medicinal jugs to get them through the struggle.

Football crowds are like the battle crowd that sat on cliffs and watched the charge of the Light Brigade "Into the valley of Death:" Theirs not to make reply, Theirs not to reason why, Theirs but to do and die.

When the field gets muddy in baseball, they stop the game. When the field gets muddy in football, the players roll around in it like boar hogs.

Boar hogs? That's the nickname of Mr. Jackson. "When I was a boy comin' up," he has said, "I was a real bad kid, the bully of the neighborhood. My older brothers said I was mean as a boar hog. 'Bo' is short for boar hog. My real name is Vincent, but nobody calls me that anymore. Even my mother calls me Bo."

Understandable that a young man might tire of even his mother referring to him in barnyard terms.

Which brings up another difference between baseball and football. In football, down on the line, insults are an expected part of the banter, insults that relate to family and birth.

In baseball, there is much less of that. And if you get close to the field, you'll hear the fielders speaking only to the pitcher. "Humma, humma, baby, c'mon, humma." Or sentiments to that effect. It's a kind of lullaby, in fact, which is why the catcher or infielder or manager makes a periodic trip to the mound, to make sure the pitcher remains awake.

The same for outfielders, like Vincent Jackson. Sometimes there is so little activity out there that they begin to doze in the summer sun.

That's why you see infielders turning and holding up one or two fingers, in order to alert the outfielders as to how many outs there are. And sometimes you'll see a manager in the dugout waving to an outfielder, trying to get his attention before he falls into deep slumber. Baseball is leisurely, if not in fact soporific. Football is, well, as the great Red Grange said, "Football is work. Baseball is fun." Besides playing football in college, Harold Grange, like Vincent Jackson, also played outfield on the baseball team.

Reached at his home in central Florida, Grange said, "People who go to games on Saturday or Sunday don't realize how much practice is involved on Monday, Tuesday, Wednesday, Thursday, and Friday. You're running plays over and over again, running up and down the field, and the coach is always giving you hell about something."

Football does have its quiet moments, and they can be confusing, especially to one not familiar with the game. P.G. Wodehouse, the English-born humorist, became a United States citizen but said, "I have never really taken to football, not continuous enough for me. They make a play, then they discuss it for awhile."

Vincent Jackson says that he would rather play games than practice, and that's what baseball is all about.

There are 16 games over a four-month period in a regular professional football season. There are 162 games over about six months in baseball. Sure, there's batting practice in baseball, but it's before a game, and guys usually kibbitz with each other and play things like pepper and chase the hat. If you're caught kibbitzing in football, they think you're nuts.

In football, you must be glum, and the crazier you are, the more serious you are seen to be. You prove this by hitting your head against a locker before a game. This is fact.

Some years ago, Jim Parker, the All-Pro lineman for the Colts, said, "In the locker room before a game I'd get to thinking real hard about what was going to happen, and I'd get to rocking, from one foot to the other. I didn't know what the hell I was doing, and guys have told me that I started knocking tables over and crashing into lockers. Jim Mutscheller, he was an end for us, he used to say that he wouldn't come near me before a game because he was afraid I'd kill him."

In baseball, when somebody jumps on you, it's usually out of elation, like Yogi Berra bounding out and hugging Don Larsen after the perfect game. In football, they pile on top of you with the possibility, if not the hope, that you may never walk a straight line again. It even happened to a Galloping Ghost. "You come to expect it," said Grange. "And if they don't jump on you, then you think they're bad football players."

Most running backs learn to read X-rays the way they learn to read defenses. "I never had my legs cut on," Jackson said. "And I plan never to go in the hospital as far as my knees are concerned."

In baseball, there is a certain lightness of spirit about the language that doesn't exist in football.

What can you say about the "blitzes" and "bombs" in football, other than to try to avoid them? But not so baseball. On a recent game-of-the-week telecast, Vin Scully noted that something was buzzing around the head of a batter, who then stepped out of the box to swat it. "That," said Scully, "must be the dreaded infield fly."

And like many mothers, Jackson's, Mrs. Florence Bond, would rather her son not play football. "My mother was against it," Jackson said a few years ago about his taking up football. "She was afraid I'd get hurt. And she'd sometimes lock me out of the house when I came home from practice."

Baseball was different. And now Vincent can always go home again.

GROUCHO CAN HEAL BASEBALL

January 16, 1969

THE BASEBALL OWNERS HAVE made no progress, like running from second base to first, in quest of a new czar. Yet it seems they are overlooking an obvious choice. Baseball history—from the Reds to the Red Sox, from Red Schoendienst to Red Ruffing to Pinky Higgins—suggests the need for Marxist leadership: Groucho Marxist.

At the mention, one steels himself for the brickbats from those dullards who say Groucho does not have the qualifications. This, if you'll pardon the French, is dropping a canard.

Groucho has spent a lifetime watching baseball and pursuing other well-rounded subjects.

His first act as commissioner, surely, would be to get baseball players to dress like they mean it.

In his book, *The Groucho Letters*, he discussed this as a P.S. to the Goodman Ace: "I saw Joe DiMaggio last night at Chasen's (Restaurant)," wrote Groucho, "and he wasn't wearing his baseball suit. This struck me as rather foolish. Suppose a ballgame broke out in the middle of the night? By the time he got into his suit the game would be over."

Baseball often has made Groucho wriggle his caterpillar eyebrows with pure delight. Take the 1940 World Series between the Yankees and the Dodgers. Groucho wrote to a friend: "I'm very happy about the World Series. I won two dollars from Miriam [Groucho's oldest daughter] or, in other words, two weeks' allowance. Miriam's allowance is becoming my chief source of income and when she grows up and flies away from the home, as they say, I don't know what I'll do for spending money."

Groucho's interest in sports goes back to childhood days in a New York City slum. In his autobiography, *Groucho and Me*, which he confesses he wrote himself, he recalled: "In my younger days, I thought I would make it as one of America's outstanding athletes. You know, the burly type like Jim Thorpe or Bob Mathias. Since I only weighed 120, stripped, I put clothes on again and abandoned the notion."

Later, Groucho tried golf. The first time was on the crowded fairways of a New York public course. "There must have been five hundred players on each hole," he wrote. "My score for the first hole was pretty good. Four golf balls whizzed past me and two got me. I finished the one hole and fled. I had read about Flanders Field during the First World War, but I never knew what it meant until I played that hole."

Once, though, he made a hole-in-one. The newspapers heard about it and a headline read: "Groucho Marx Joins the Immortals." The next day, with photographers abounding, Marx was asked to replay the hole. He had a 21, "and that was only because I was putting unusually well," he said.

Getting back to the czarship of baseball, Groucho would be no stranger to the administrative end. In the Marx Brothers movie, *Horse Fathers*, he played Professor Quincy Adams Wagstaff, a recently appointed college president. Talking to two of his professors, Groucho says, "The trouble is, we're neglecting football for education.... Where would this college be without football? Have we got a stadium?"

Yes, replied one of the professors. Groucho asks, "Have we got a college?" Yes. "Well," decides Groucho, "we can't support both. Tomorrow we start tearing down the college." But president, asks a faculty member, where will the students sleep?

"Where they always slept," states the president. "In the classroom."

In *A Day At the Races*, Groucho plays Dr. Hugo Z. Hackenbush, quack veterinarian. At one point in the movie he gives a huge pill to a sore horse and advises the steed, "Take one of these every half mile and call me if there's any change."

So it is apparent to even the most jaundiced eye that Groucho Marx is the experienced man baseball needs. But, of course, they cannot ask him to take the post. He would accept only if it were refused him. "I would never join a club," Groucho has said, "that would want me for a member."

• • •

Bowie Kuhn, not Groucho Marx, was named the next commissioner of baseball.

RAIN CHECK

July 7, 1972

RAINING HARDER. POCKETS OF puddles now cover the slick infield tarpaulin. Little hope that a ballgame will be played today.

The summer rain started earlier in the morning. There was a sudden, ominous appearance of dark clouds. It brought a shift of wind and bend of tree. Then, in rapid orchestration, a rumble of the kettledrum, a rise of the snare, a boom of the bass drum, and an ultimate clash of cymbals. Crackle of lightning. Rain.

How quickly cheeriness can become gloom. Bright prospects of a ballgame today swiftly drowning.

Yet there remains hope for the sun. The ballplayers come to the park, hustling from bus to car with newspaper covering their heads as they hop and dodge puddles. They do not look up to the stadium roof and see flags heavy with rain, losing the struggle to flap in the wind.

Taciturn vendors and sullen ticket sellers are there. Some fans, with optimism as implacable as the rain, arrive.

Umbrellas pop up in the stands like mushrooms. Another jolt of lightning and a man with his son seated next to him lowers his black umbrella, as if he is pulling a bedcover tighter over their frightened heads.

One man under a poncho sits alone in the saturated bleachers. There is only a dark cavity where his face might be. A wet imitation of the Grim Reaper.

Rain everywhere. The big black scoreboard is blacker for the wash. The outfield is soaked. Cops stand outside the dugout, their black slickers glistening in the downpour.

Lights are turned on; an ersatz sun which brings no relief from the rain. But the tarpaulin's puddles are now sprinkled with the stars. The geometric railings give a glassiness to the stands.

A few half-dressed players with shower shoes stand on the dugout bench, since the floor is already filling with water.

"Can you swim?" one asks another. "If not we'll have to cut you."

The batboy has had to run from one dugout to another. In that short desperate flight he has become matted with rain. He had to slosh through the sea of mud and water in front of the dugouts. He comes dripping, clattering, and laughing breathlessly out of the rain. He brings into the dugout a smell of wet wool, shakes himself like a spaniel.

A couple of players return to playing cards in the quiet of the clubhouse. Pitchers will wonder what a rainout will mean to their mechanical routine and rotation. A slumping batter is thankful for a day of respite.

A second-line player is prepared for a drenching of ego in an unusual way, if the game goes on. He will probably be in the starting lineup since the manager does not want to risk injury to a star on a poor field.

But a team in a hot streak is afraid the rain may dampen its momentum.

And one remembers the Boston Braves of 1948, with the saying "Spahn and Sain and pray for rain." (One wonders how Vern Bickford, the Braves' third starter that championship season, felt about that rhyme. Was it like water off a duck's back?) And in Chicago that season the last-place Cubs had a soggy saying, too: "Kush and Rush and pray for slush." (The Cubs didn't have a third pitcher, with or without tender feelings.)

Raining, raining, raining. The hands of the scoreboard clock are seemingly sodden now, for it's an hour past game time. And still no game. The home team is forever reluctant to give up the ship, and the prospects of a miracle: sun and a good crowd. But soon the announcement: sorry, no game today.

The several thousand fans boo. But boo whom? The management? The public address announcer? The turbulent gods? The snipping of hope?

And yet in their wet pockets these fans can clutch a rain check, a soggy but palpable symbol of a better day ahead. The rain check is a passport to sunshine.

About the Author

Ira Berkow, a sports columnist and feature writer for *The New York Times* for more than 25 years, shared the Pulitzer Prize for national reporting in 2001 and was a finalist for the Pulitzer for commentary in 1988. He also was a reporter for the *Minneapolis Tribune* and a columnist for Newspaper Enterprise Association. He is the author of 20 books, including the bestsellers *Red: A Biography of Red Smith* and *Maxwell Street: Survival in a Bazaar*, and, most recently, *Summers in the Bronx: Attila the Hun and Other Yankee Stories*. His work has frequently been cited in the prestigious anthology series, *Best American Sports Writing*, as well as the 1999 anthology *Best American Sports Writing of the Century*. He holds a bachelor's degree from Miami University (Ohio) and a master's degree from Northwestern University's Medill School of Journalism, and has been honored with distinguished professional achievement awards from both schools. In 2009 he was inducted into the International Jewish Sports Hall of Fame and also received an Honorary Doctorate of Humane Letters from Roosevelt University in Chicago. Mr. Berkow lives in New York City.